ONE DOG

AND HIS MAN

MARJORIE QUARTON

For Diana

First published in book form in 1984 by
The Blackstaff Press
3 Galway Park, Dundonald, Belfast BT16 0AN

Some of these stories first appeared in
Working Sheepdog News

Printed in Northern Ireland by
Belfast Litho Printers Ltd

British Library Cataloguing in Publication Data
Quarton, Marjorie
One dog and his man.
1. Dogs – Anecdotes, facetiae, satire, etc.
I. Title
636.7   SF426.2

ISBN 0 85640 319 9

Marjorie Quarton was born and brought up in Co. Tipperary where she and her husband now farm at Ballycommon. She has been a sheepdog breeder for some fifteen years and is a regular contributor to *Working Sheepdog News*, the *Farmers' Journal* and *Farmers' Monthly*. She is the author of *The Farm Dog – a Beginner's Guide* and is currently working on a new book about Border collies.

BORED

In Coolcoffin, where I live, nearly every dog you meet is called Shep.

'What else would you call a dog?' says the Boss when the Missis asked him what name would he give me.

One thing I have that the other Sheps haven't is a number, 80645. It doesn't do me any good that I can see, but me Mammy told me I should be proud of it and I am.

I don't remember me Mammy that well, though I remember her biting our ears for being bold. I think it's a pity my Boss's Mammy didn't bite his ears more when he was a little 'un; she might have put some sense into him.

I wasn't born in Coolcoffin at all but in Wicklow, the other side of Ireland. The Boss saw us advertised in the *Farmers' Journal* and he took the notion to buy me because me Mammy and me Da was champions.

It was a bad day for me, four years ago, when I came to Coolcoffin.

For the first year of me life I hardly saw the light of day as I was kept shut up in an old shed. I got as much food as I could eat and plenty of dry straw for a bed, but it was a dull old life all the same.

When I got big, the Boss started taking me for the cows and I began to work. It came natural to me, and I thought I was doing the finest when the boss took it into his head to train me. That came to nothing because he didn't know how to do it, and anyway I could run faster than he could, so he soon gave up.

From then on, I did as I liked. I brought the cows in and rounded up the sheep; I got the hens in for the Missis as well.

The Missis is mad about me. She says I'm almost human, which she means for a compliment, the poor harmless woman.

That's my story up to now, and I suppose I'll spend the rest of me days here in County Galway, tied to the wheel of an old trap.

My friend Dolly has been here longer than I have. She is great for barking and chasing cars. She didn't catch one yet, but she keeps trying.

I heard the Boss talking about a sheepdog trial that's to be held at Oughterard on Sunday. I don't know what a sheepdog trial is, but I do wish I could go to it. Whatever it is, it would be more interesting than sitting here with nothing to do only scratch meself and chew this old wheel.

Ah, it's a dog's life at times.

SORRY

When the Boss came home from the trial at Oughterard, the Missis asked him was it as good as he expected.

''Deed it wasn't then,' says the Boss. 'I was at it all day and I saw nothing my Shep and Dolly couldn't do. I'm taking Shep to the next trial there is.'

I was sorry Dolly wasn't going, but she had to stay at home on account of her pups. Of course, they're my pups too – at least I think they are.

On Sunday, the Boss and the Missis and me went off to the trial in the car. The Missis took her knitting and *Ireland's Own*; the Boss took a stick. I went in the boot, with only the spare wheel for company.

When we got to the trial, I lepped out of the boot and said 'Hello' to the first dog I saw. He stripped his teeth.

'I'm Risp,' says he, 'I won on the telly. You watch your step.'

I thought it wasn't the time to ask him for his autograph, so I got under our car, had a good scratch and went to sleep.

It was in the novice class we were. The Boss pulled me out from under the car and off we went to the start. I wasn't a bit scared. I knew all me commands – Come in, Get out, Lie down damn you, Get up, G'way outa that and G'home ye divil.

There were only four little sheep, and I wasn't long

bringing them, I can tell you! The Boss looked mad, but maybe he wasn't. I whipped the sheep around him, and ran them back to the far end. Then I heard a big shout, and the Boss was wanting them back again. He'd changed his mind, and wanted me to put them in a pen. I got them back after a while – they did gallop! And I put them into the pen as well. Then the Boss changed his mind again and let them out of the pen after all me bother.

I thought I had the trial won, but they said I did something wrong – I forget what.

After that, I had to go back in the boot so I missed the rest. I don't think much of these old trials, so I don't... and I was sick over the spare wheel going home... the Boss says he is taking Dolly next time.

INTERESTED

I have found out that I have Paper! I never knew that before, but it's right. It's a blue yoke with me name and number, me Mammy and me Da, and the Boss as well, but he's in small letters.

Dolly has no papers – she's only half a purebred. The Boss used to say pedigrees weren't worth the paper they were written on, and he could give names to his dog without sending money to any society. That's all changed since he was talking to some fellers at the sheepdog trial.

Dolly's pups are called Rover, Spot, Darkie and Ginger. They are all brown with white spots and long ears. This is funny, because Dolly is all black and I'm black with a white collar and legs and a white stripe down me face.

One day, the Boss let the pups out in the field to see would they bring the sheep. They didn't bring them at all; they chased them through the ditch and away to the mountain. I had to fetch them back, and a right job I had of it. Dolly came too, but she just stood and barked.

At dinnertime, the Boss says to the Missis, 'Look at Shep, he's the only dog around here that's any use.'

'Of course he is,' says the Missis, 'he's the only one with papers.'

The Boss says, 'Begod, you're right. I'll get another pedigree dog the next time.'

The same day, the Boss sent away to Donegal for a new puppy. He wrote a letter answering an advert for a pedigree bitch pup, registration optional.

'What does "optional" mean?' asks the Missis.

'It means you have to have it,' says the Boss. 'They didn't teach you much at that old convent if you don't know that.'

He went off that evening on his bike to post the letter in Coolcoffin. When he was there he called at the pub and arranged to give Rover, Spot, Darkie and Ginger to a man who was lonely.

He was late back because the bike refused to carry him home. He makes out they are treacherous things after pubs.

On Saturday, he brought home the puppy from the railway in an orange box. 'LIVE PUPPY, THIS WAY UP', it said.

She's called Jess, and she has pink papers, which are even better than blue, they say. When the Missis let her out of the box, she went under the dresser, and screeched for her Mammy.

'You wouldn't think a pedigree dog would make such a noise, would you?' says the Missis.

'There's no need to shout,' says the Boss, shouting himself above the noise. 'Poor little thing, she's hungry.' Dolly and me couldn't believe our ears. We thought he must be going off his head. The Missis went off to get some milk, and the Boss sat down to read his new book on sheepdog training.

These are very strange times we live in.

GETTING OUT OF THE WAY

My wheel, what I'm tied to, is part of an old trap. When I came to the farm, there was an ass to pull it, but he died. Now the Boss has a car and a bike. Martin, the young lad, is after getting a job away in Tuam, so he needs the car. That means the Boss rides the bike and the Missis stays at home. She was inclined to be cribbing about it, so the Boss bought a small pony to pull the trap. The idea was for her to drive it, but she never did.

My wheel, where I live, isn't what it was. I have three spokes eaten right through and two half-way. Well, I've been tied to it for three years so you couldn't blame me for edging me teeth on it now and then. Anyone would.

Jess is three months old now and doing well. So she should, with more champions in her pedigree than there are islands in Lough Corrib. All of a sudden, the Missis took the notion to take her to the vet for injections agin distemper.

I was all wrong about distemper. I thought it was stuff the Boss put on the cowshed wall. He spilled it and I walked in it – you can see me pawmarks yet on the flagstones. They are pink and I think they look lovely.

Now they tell me distemper is a disease. It's terrible confusing altogether.

The Missis yoked the pony herself, and remembered to untie me before she took the trap out. Jess was in a box on the seat. Just as the Missis drove away, Dolly ran out barking like she always does, the pony shied, the bad wheel went over a stone and that was the end of it. It all broke up, the trap turned over and the Missis and Jess fell out.

The Boss came flying out of the house when he heard the commotion.

'Is the pup all right?' says he, picking up the box, with Jess yelping inside.

'I think she is,' says the Missis, getting up shakily, 'but I'm not. My knee is bleeding, and I think my finger is broke.'

I thought it would be a good idea not to be around when they looked at the wheel, so I went off for a long walk on me own.

HUNGRY

The Boss talks about training Jess soon. She's getting big now and very good-looking, although Dolly doesn't agree with me about this.

The Missis thought she might train her herself, but the Boss said no because he says a pedigree dog will never work for a woman. I know that's not right because I work for the Missis meself. Still I suppose even the Boss could be wrong sometimes.

He is learning how to train Jess from books. He got five of them from the library and he has them all read twice. I was in the kitchen with the Missis when he came home with a new one called *Breeding and Training Sheepdogs For Profit And Pleasure*. He sat down and read aloud – '"Always speak to your dog in language he can understand."'

'Why, you always do that,' says the Missis. 'Sometimes they can hardly get under the henhouse fast enough.'

'That's all over,' says the Boss. '"A tone of quiet authority should be used" – quiet, mind you, "and the results will surprise you."'

'They might, I suppose,' says the Missis. 'Who wrote the book?'

'It doesn't give his name,' says the Boss, 'calls himself "Come Bye". It says here inside the cover – "Come Bye exhibits a unique grasp of canine psychology." That means he understands these old dogs.' He went on – '"A properly balanced diet is essential."'

'What's wrong with spuds and new milk, I should like to know?' asks the Missis. 'Shep looks well on them.'

'It isn't Shep I worry about, it's young Jess,' says the Boss.

About a week after that he came home from town with a four-stone bag with a dog's head on it.

'*Collywobbles*,' asks the Missis, 'whatever are they?'

'Balanced diet,' says the Boss, slitting the bag.

'They look more like brown wellingtons minced,' says the Missis, and she read off the bag: '"Just add water for meaty morsels, smothered with gutsy gravy." You'll poison the creatures!'

'"Deed I won't then,' says the Boss. 'It's a quare name but great stuff. There's some for little 'uns too, called "Pup-Slup".'

I've had a plate of Collywobbles for me dinner every day since. The smell is a bit funny, but the taste is all right.

Still and all, I miss me spuds.

THIRSTY

The Boss is getting a magazine from England every month now. It has a picture of me on the cover, or maybe he's one of my relations. They are mostly white-collar workers like meself.

The Boss began talking about P.R.A.* after reading it. I think it stands for 'Partly Reduced Activity', or something like that. Anyway it means I might go blind. I don't think I will, because the Boss and the Missis both need glasses and I don't.

One day, the Boss says to the Missis, 'I'm taking Shep to Dublin to have his eyes tested.'

The Missis just stared at him. She says, 'Now I *know* you're out of your mind. Dublin's 150 miles. What's wrong with Mr Finnegan in Coolcoffin?'

'It has to be Dublin,' says the Boss. 'Jim Dolan and meself will go next week.'

We set off early one morning in Jim's van. I went in the back with Ben, his dog. We drove for hours, and got very bored and thirsty. At last we got to Dublin, and a man had a look at our eyes and said they were all right.

It was after that the trouble started. The Boss and Jim set off for home, but stopped the van after a few minutes, and went into a pub for a pint. Ben and me waited and waited. We had a small fight, just to pass the time, then

* Progressive Retinal Atrophy

11

we went to sleep. When we woke, it was dark, and Jim and the Boss were climbing into the van. They drove off in great humour, singing 'Galway Bay'.

We drove for two hours or more, and then Jim says to the Boss, 'Try and see the name of this big town we're coming to.'

'Wexford,' says the Boss.

'G'way,' says Jim, 'it can't be.'

But it was, and it's a long, long way from Wexford to Galway, and another forty miles on to Coolcoffin.

We were home for breakfast next day. I never saw the Missis really angry before, but this time I think the Boss would have come under the henhouse with me if he would have fitted. It'll be a long time before he goes to Dublin again, I think.

SAD

It's a sad story I have to tell this time. My friend Dolly is dead. This is the way it happened. On Sunday, the Boss and the Missis went to a match. They left Dolly loose to mind the place. Me and Jess was tied up in the shed.

When they were gone, Martin came home with two friends. The house was locked up, but we heard them talking out in the haybarn. They were smoking too – the Boss wouldn't have allowed that.

When they'd gone away, I smelled smoke. Jess and me was desperate scared. We whined and howled, but Dolly was barking at cars on the road and didn't hear us.

Just then, a car came fast down our road, Dolly ran out, barking, and it went over her and killed her stone dead.

The driver mustn't have known Dolly, for he was very sorry, and stopped and brought her into the yard. Then he saw the straw starting to burn in the barn. There's a big water tank outside, so he got a bucket and put the fire out. He was just finished when the Boss landed back.

Dolly's funeral was to have been that evening at the river, but the Missis said that wouldn't do. She said Dolly had given her life stopping the car, so the man would put out the fire, and save the house from burning down, and Jess and me and the hens from a horrible death.

'Dolly deserves a proper grave,' says the Missis to the Boss, 'and it wouldn't do you a bit of harm to dig one.

You could put up a stone saying "SHE WAS FAITHFUL", like the dog in the book.'

'"SHE WAS USELESS" would be more like it,' says the Boss. 'You soon changed your mind about Dolly, didn't you? Only last week you were giving her who-began-it with the sweeping brush.'

However, the Missis usually gets her way in the end, and Dolly got a fine grave in the garden.

The Missis cried, but the Boss didn't – not when I was there anyway.

'OH NO'

As if it wasn't bad enough losing me old friend, I nearly lost another one the very next week. That was the day Jess killed a hen.

The Boss and the Missis was gone out in the car. I was tied up but Jess was loose, and she made short work of that hen.

'You're for it when the Boss comes home, my girl,' says I. 'Your pink papers won't save you then.'

'Why?' says Jess. 'I only did what they do themselves. I just killed one old hen, and pulled off her feathers, and took out her insides. They often do it.'

'They make a tidier job,' says I.

Somewhere in the sheepdog book the Boss is always reading aloud it says, 'If you feel annoyed with your dog, never show it. Keep cool and calm.' I think the Boss had forgotten that bit. Anyone could see he was annoyed when he saw what was left of the hen. He was just grabbing Jess when she got free, and ran straight out onto the road.

'I used to think those pedigree dogs wouldn't touch hens,' says the Missis, gathering up the bits.

'I used to think a Wiston Cap* was a woollen yoke to wear on your head,' says the Boss. 'You learn better,' he says.

* Wiston Cap – the Red Rum of sheepdog trials.

15

I thought he wouldn't mind about Jess running away, but I was wrong as usual. First he walked all the way to Coolcoffin, calling and whistling with his special whistle. It is a red one with a string on it, so that he can get it back if he swallows it. He took me with him in case Jess would sooner come to me than him. He had a point there. As he walked, he kept saying he'd murder Jess when he found her. Then he reported her lost to the Guards, and put an ad in the *Coolcoffin Courier*.

Then we walked home, and there was Jess in the yard. You never can tell with the Boss. There wasn't another word about murdering Jess. He just calmly and coolly tied her up. He must have remembered that old book.

MAD

One day, the Missis saw an ad in the *Farmers' Journal*: 'Scottish lady would like to spend Christmas on Irish farm, where own well-trained collie welcome,' it read.

'She could tell you how to train Jess,' says the Missis.

'I don't want no woman to tell me anything,' says the Boss. He was in a bad humour.

The Missis got her way as usual, and she was awful busy getting ready for the Christmas and the visitor. Even so, she found time to groom me and Jess. She shined us up rightly with a Brillo pad.

I was around when Miss Cairngorm arrived. She had a big, hairy, pale brown dog with her.

'I know you'll all love Mr Teazie-Weazie,' says she, hugging him.

'We will, I suppose,' says the Boss. 'Tie him up there in the shed.'

'Oh no,' says Miss Cairngorm, 'he's used to a centrally-heated kennel. He must sleep in my room.'

Meanwhile, I asked Mr Teazie-Weazie, 'Are you a Border Collie then?'

'Wouldn't be seen dead with one,' says he. 'No, I'm the Lassie type.'

'Oh, beg pardon,' says I, 'I thought you were a Laddie. Still, I suppose it takes all sorts.'

Miss Cairngorm heard us growling. 'Another thing,'

says she, 'I don't want my dog to associate with farm animals. It's unhealthy.' With that she led him indoors.

'Mongrel!' says Teazie over his shoulder as he went.

Next time I saw him, I was just finishing my Christmas dinner in the cowshed when he walked in.

'Bit chilly for eating outdoors,' he remarked.

Now, I wasn't tied up, so I said, 'Who did you call a mongrel yesterday?' Mr Teazie-Weazie squinted at me with his little eyes down his long nose.

'Ah, that was a joke,' says he. 'I am proud of my ancestry, that's all. Do you realise how many times my father won a green star?'

'Once in a blue moon, I'd say,' says I, 'unless there was only himself in the class.'

Well, I'll say this for the useless eejit, he could fight, and soon we were rolling in what the *Farmers' Journal* calls slurry. Cow and pig, mixed. I loosed my hold of Teazie-Weazie to get a better grip, and the next thing I knew he was gone, yelping and yowling, back to the house, through the kitchen, up the stairs and, for all I know, into Miss Cairngorm's bed.

I never did find out because, since then, I've been tied to the leg of an old turnip pulper in the back yard.

I thought the Boss would beat me, but he was hardly vexed at all. Of course, he didn't have to clean up the mess.

SNEAKY

Jess and me lived in a nice cosy stable all winter because, now that the cows were dry and the ewes near lambing, there was very little work for me to do.

Jess doesn't work at any time. She creeps about, a long way off, looking very keen and clever, but really, she's scared. The Boss and the Missis don't know this. They think she will make a champion some day.

'When she's reared a litter of pups, that's when she'll start to work right,' says the Missis.

One day, the vet came, testing cattle, and I was working them.

'That's a great dog,' says the vet, 'what happened to the little bitch you bought?'

'I'll show her to you,' says the Boss. 'She's a lovely mover, but not quite ready for serious training.'

He took the vet into our stable to see Jess.

'I'm going to breed some champions off this lady,' says the Boss, 'I'm sending her across the water to the International winner.'

'I think you're too late,' says the vet, 'she's already in whelp.'

'Oh no,' says the Boss, 'I know she got stout, but that's the balanced diet.'

'It is not,' says the vet, 'it's pups.'

I was standing beside the Boss looking harmless, but I

thought it might be time to go away. The Boss is hasty sometimes.

Two weeks after that, Jess had five pups – real smashers. The Missis says to the Boss, 'I don't know why you're so vexed over this. Shep is well bred, and a great worker.'

'Maybe,' says the Boss, 'but he never won a trial, and I wanted big money for those pups.'

You'd hardly believe what he's going to do now. He's sending me to be trained for trials to a man that makes a business of it, so that he can ask more for the pups.

What makes me laugh is thinking how him and the Missis is going to have to run after the sheep when I'm not there.

I only hope the Boss runs some fat off himself and some sense into his head.

PROUD

This isn't the first time the Boss thought he'd make a trial dog of me. There was the time he ran me in a novice class (that's never mentioned now). Then another time he thought it would do me good to watch famous dogs at work and he took me to the trial at the Four Roads.

I got talking to a dog called Mac when I got bored with watching.

'My Boss is here since eleven this morning,' says I, 'and it's getting dark. I think he's going crazy.'

'Not at all,' says Mac, 'it's sick he is. He has the trial bug, and it's worse than distemper.'

'Oh God, that's terrible,' says I. 'Will he die of it?'

'Indeed and he won't,' says Mac. 'My feller's had it for years and he's no different. The trouble is, there's no cure for it and it's catching.'

I was very sorry for the Boss. It's a shame when you think it could have been avoided if he'd got an injection from the vet when he was young.

Well, Mac was right. The Boss still has the trial bug and the Missis has caught it too.

I never thought that, at my time of life, I'd be taking up a part-time job. But here I am, at Mr O'Brien's place, being trained for trial work.

Mr O'Brien's sheep are racing fit, ready to run for their lives. I'm doubtful whether any human teeth would make much of a leg of that mutton. Mr O'Brien has two very good trial dogs going to trials every Sunday, and two more students like me. One is called Finn, he ran in a few trials already, the other is called Toby. He is a wild kind of a yoke and knows as much about farm work as a cow does about a holiday.

I asked Finn what he was doing there after I'd seen him at work. 'I'm developing a pear-shaped outrun,' says he.

'That's bad,' says I, 'did you see the vet about it?'

'I hope that's meant for a joke,' says Finn with a growl, so I said no more, and I still don't know what he meant.

Mr O'Brien didn't like me at first. 'Too headstrong,' says he, 'overruns, comes in too close, lacks the correct approach.' There was a whole pile more, but it's doggerel to me.

I got my chance one day, when we were taking it in turns to go around the sheep. Toby slipped his collar and made straight for them, going like the clappers. The sheep took one look, and away with them, heading for the fence. Toby had frightened the souls out of them once or twice before. Straight through the wire they went with Toby after them, and onto the next farm where there were ewes with lambs. When Mr O'Brien caught Toby, he shook him until his brains would have rattled if he'd had any. Then he took me and we sorted the sheep out. He's easier to work with than the Boss, because he knows what he's trying to do.

When Finn said we were going to run in a nursery, I thought there wouldn't be much room for running, and we might frighten the childer, but I learned lately to say nothing when I don't understand, and it's lucky I did.

Mr O'Brien loaded up Finn and me in a little trailer he has, with his name on it, and away we went.

When we stopped, we were at a hilly place, and I saw there was a trial on. Then I saw the Boss coming, so I ran up to him and licked his hand.

'Get away, you ould villain, you,' says the Boss. I could tell he was delighted to see me. With the Boss, it isn't so much what he says as how he says it.

'You'll notice a big change in Shep,' says Mr O'Brien.

'I do,' says the Boss, 'he's much cleaner.' Then they had a long chat and I watched a few dogs running. I enjoyed myself to pieces watching some of them. Some wouldn't lie down, others wouldn't get up, and one dog ran the sheep off the course, up the road and out of sight.

'These trials are a howl, aren't they?' says I to Finn.

'You might be howling before night,' says Finn, 'it's your turn next.'

I'd learned a lot since the Boss ran me in a trial last year. I went nice and handy, and minded what Mr O'Brien taught me. When it was over, they said I had it won!

Mr O'Brien told the Boss he would give him £500 for me.

'I want a thousand,' says the Boss. I was glad I wasn't to be sold, so I put me nose in his hand.

'Go to Hell, you silly ould divil,' says the Boss. It was grand to see him again and know how much he thought about me.

The latest news is that the Boss is coming to Mr O'Brien's place to be trained himself, because he wants to run me in trials and I'm after learning different commands.

That'll be a howl if you like.

FRUSTRATED

Mr O'Brien is running me in trials regular now, and twice a week the Boss comes here to be trained so he can run me himself. He's not good at it, any pup would learn quicker, but we aren't getting on too badly.

One day, the Boss was practising with another dog, and I was talking to one of Mr O'Brien's dogs, Kep.

Kep says, 'What a pity your Boss couldn't think of a better name than Shep for a good trial dog like you.'

'If he had to name me now, I might be Coolcoffin Cap or Coolcoffin Coon,' says I. 'I'd sooner be Shep. Anyway, I have a number too.'

'Everyone has a number,' says Kep, 'but I have letters after me name. R.O.M.* What do you think of that?'

'What does it stand for?' says I.

'I don't know,' says Kep, 'but I do know it cost my Boss £50 to get them for me.'

'Perhaps it stands for "Rich Or Mad",' says I.

Now, while we were talking, the Boss was working a dog belonging to Mr O'Brien, rounding up ducks, and putting them into a pen. Both the Boss and the dog found this a great strain on the temper. I never worked ducks, but I was well used to putting in the hens for the Missis at home, and you need a cool head for that. When the Boss tried it when the Missis was sick, we finished up with me under the henhouse, the Boss at the pub, and the hens

* Registered on Merit

24

roosting in the sally trees by the river.

When the ducks were penned, Mr O'Brien says to the Boss, 'I can teach you no more; it's up to yourself from this on. You have one of the best dogs in the country, and I only wish you would sell him to me.'

'I have a better one at home,' says the Boss, 'when she has her pups reared and comes to her best.'

He's in for a disappointment, I'm afraid.

When we landed home, the Boss could talk of nothing but how he penned Mr O'Brien's ducks. He thought ducks would be just the thing for Jess.

She has her pups reared and she sometimes gives me a turn with the hens but she dreads sheep and the sheep know it. As for cattle, I still have everything to do with them.

The Boss has a neighbour called Jamesy Quinn that he goes to the pub with. He's a bit like the Boss – cross as a cat, but decent with it.

One day, the Boss says to Jamesy, 'Would you ever give me a loan of those old ducks of yours till I get Jess going around them.'

'Fair enough,' says Jamesy, 'but don't upset them because they're laying and my Missis will eat me if anything happens them.'

'My dogs won't hurt them,' says the Boss, 'they have the best of breeding.'

He let the ducks out of their crate in the middle of the big field, and sent Jess around them. The ducks didn't know Jess, so they were very nervous and began to quack and flap their wings. Jess was delighted because she'd found something that was afraid of her instead of the other way round, and she began to chase them. The ducks flew up in the air, and the Boss let a roar at me to head them off. I'm fairly fast, but I can't run as fast as a duck can fly, and I was still well behind when they reached the river and set off swimming downstream at top speed. I

jumped in and swam after them a long way, under the railway bridge and nearly to the mill. Then I said to meself that Jamesy Quinn's ducks weren't worth drowning for, and I was getting very tired.

I climbed out of the river, leaving the ducks still heading for the Atlantic, and took a short cut back to the big field. Long before I got there, I heard the Boss and Jamesy shouting at each other, so I kept at the back of the hedge, and went home to see could I find the Missis.

The Missis was very surprised to see me so wet, and she rubbed me dry with an old vest belonging to the Boss, and let me sit in the kitchen.

We never did any work with ducks since.

LYING LOW

Not long ago, the Boss put an ad in the *Farmers' Journal*. It read, 'Five Border Collie pups for sale. Sire leading trial winner. Dam potential champion. Unregistered owing to misunderstanding. Send S.A.E. for details.'

Very soon people began to arrive in the yard and go away with one of our pups. Soon there was just the one left, Tiny.

Tiny is a ringing divil. He stands in the middle of the kitchen floor, as bold as a pig, not afraid of anything or anybody. The Boss says he's too small but the Missis is fond of Tiny, and she told the Boss that even he must have been small when he was eight weeks old.

One day lately, the Missis went to Jamesy Quinn's house for a few hours. The family is coming back from America, and the Missis was giving Mrs Quinn a hand putting everything in order. When she'd gone, the Boss set off for Coolcoffin on his bike. Tiny followed him onto the road, and I could hear the Boss trying to hunt him home. After a few minutes, Tiny came flying back into the yard with the Boss running after him.

Now, Tiny is very brave, but he knows when it's wisest not to be caught, and he ran into the big shed and went under the old binder in the corner.

The Boss bent down, snapping his fingers and saying, 'Come on then, good little feller!' Then he shook his fist and shouted, 'Come out of that till I skin you!' Tiny stayed where he was.

The Boss is fairly stout and not young, but he doesn't like to be beaten, so he got down on his hands and knees and began to creep under the binder.

It was a warm day, so he hadn't his jacket on, and the next minute the back of his shirt caught in the underside of the binder. The Boss couldn't move forward or back, and he was afraid he'd tear his shirt. He did make a noise! Tiny sat, just out of reach, with his head on one side, watching him.

When the Missis came back from Jamesy Quinn's house, she heard the Boss roaring murder and soon found him and set him free. To make matters worse, he saw her trying to keep from laughing.

Tiny and me spent the rest of the day under the hen-house.

IN CONTROL

The Boss had teethaches cruel bad a while ago, so he went to Galway and had them all pulled. He says they never pained him since. Now he has new teeth which he takes everywhere in his pocket. He has to wear them when he wants to blow his whistle, so he put them in for the big trial at Ballydonald.

It was supposed to be a good chance for me, because some of the best handlers were over at the Welsh National, and another had gone to Lisdoonvarna for the week-end

I suppose I was lucky to win that trial. I do best if not too much is said to me, and the Boss had to let me pen the sheep quite on me own because his whistle had got mixed up with his false teeth so he could only splutter. Very often, he gets edgy at the pen, so I do too and so do the sheep.

They laugh at this old trial bug, and indeed it's a holy fright in some ways and the vets still can't cure it, but it's done the Boss a lot of good. I haven't felt his stick for a year, and I haven't felt his boot for two.

We won the trial very easy and the Boss was solid delighted. He won a shepherd's crook and some money as well.

When it was over, two strangers came along, and they were talking to the Boss for a long time. I wasn't taking much notice, but I did hear the Boss say, 'I want to be on the Irish team. It's me heart's desire. I won't rest till I make that team.'

I thought he'd do well to get on because the National Trial is over for this year, I don't get any younger, and I still don't see him winning anything at all with Jess. He's tried and tried, for hours at a time, to train her, and still she won't even sit down when she's told. The Missis has done much better. She has Jess trained to get the clothes pegs out of the bag, one by one, and hand them to her as they are wanted. When the Boss found this out, instead of being pleased, I thought he was going to burst with rage. He made the Missis promise not to teach me anything at all.

sman
a num-
in recent
cause fires within
son.

Prisoners' hit out,page 5

and role
tar Lynch

in a
nture

a new
Daniel

shed his
n "Cal",
ma school

e's desert
n director
d thought

Ocean for

a remote
frica.
as not yet
t available

By Neil Johnston

For the 24-year-old Newry man who began acting in amateur drama productions in his home town, it is yet another high point in his brief but remarkable stage career.

Since making "Cal" he has appeared in a West End production of a Chekhov play and last year he toured America with the Royal Shakespeare Company playing the part of Smike in their much acclaimed stage adaptation of "Nicholas Nickleby".

Three years ago he was an unknown drama student - now he is one of the hottest properties in British acting.

He can be seen in "Cal", the film from the Bernard MacLaverty novel in which he plays opposite Helen Mirren, when it is screened by Channel Four on the night of February 26.

an
end
the ge...
have suffe...
My hand, a...
happier Land. G...
mum.

BINGHAM, AGNES — ...
regretted by her Daught...
Isabell Husband Sammy, and
Grand-daughter Jillian. Those
we love don't go away, they
walk beside us every day. God
Bless you Mum.

BINGHAM, AGNES — Deeply
regretted by her Daughter Janet
Husband Greg and Grandsons.
Your restless days are over,
your sleepless nights are past.
God put his arms around you,
and gave you peace at last.

C...
Joseph...
Hill, Gir...
late reside...
day), at 2.3...
Parish Chu...
private. Fami...
please. — Deep...
her sorrowing
Family Circle.

COPY TIMES FOR NOTIC[
APPEARING ON THIS PA[

Births, Marriages, In-Memoriams, Thanks
Wedding Notices, etc. should reach us by 5 p.m
the day prior to publication (Saturday 12 noon
for Monday's paper).

FUNERAL & SYMPATHY NOTICES

Monday-Friday Editions
Sympathy Notices can be
accepted up to 10.00 a.m. on
the morning of publication
and main Funeral Notices up
to 10.30 a.m.

Saturday Editions
Both sympathy and main
funeral notices should reach
us before 10 a.m. on Saturday
mornings.

As all the above times are the latest times we would
ask you please to have copy with us as soon as
possible prior to these times.

CLASSIFIEDS. TEL. BELFAST 22129[

MORTIFIED

The Boss's son, Martin, was working in England for a good while. He left home after him and the Boss had a row over the straw going on fire in the barn the day Dolly was killed. He left his job after six months, and came home. Since then he's been here, working on the farm, which means the Boss has plenty of time to spend with us dogs and at trials. Tiny is going to be good, but if Jess is a champion, I'm an Alsatian.

When Martin came home, his hair was away below his shoulders. It's bright red and curly, and he looked a holy show. The Boss ordered him to get it cut but he took no notice. The Missis says, 'Ah, leave the poor lad alone, it's trendy he is. They have to follow the fashion.' The Boss said no more.

The Boss's hair is a patchy grey, blue merle I suppose you'd call it if he were a dog. He hasn't any on top, but that doesn't matter, because you hardly ever see him without his hat. Anyway, it grew and grew and the Missis says, 'For the love of God, will you get a haircut, you'd frighten the crows.'

'Not at all,' says the Boss, 'it's the fashion. I'll cut it off when Martin does.'

The next Sunday, the Boss took me to a trial. 'I won't come unless you do something about your hair,' says the Missis.

'Don't so,' says the Boss.

I came second in the trial, and afterwards I saw the same two men that was at Ballydonald talking to the Boss. This time I listened and, if you'll believe me, they were asking him to go on TV with me! I knew all about the old programme. It's called *One Dog and His Man* – I think – and the Boss and the Missis wouldn't miss it for anything.

After they'd been talking, the men moved away and I heard one say, 'That old character will make the show, with his long hair and his collarless shirt and his gumboots. What a laugh!'

When the Boss got home he told the Missis, and he told her the men were coming to take pictures of us all.

'What? With you looking like that! I'd be ashamed,' says the Missis.

The next morning, Martin appeared with his hair an inch long all over. Then the Boss and the Missis went to Galway. When they came back, you'd hardly know them. The Missis' hair was cut and curly all over, like a poodle. She had a new coat and red boots. As for the Boss, if I hadn't recognised his scent, I'd have growled at him. He had a tweed hat, no hair to be seen anywhere except a few bristles round his ears, a green anorak, fawn trousers and brown shoes. He didn't look happy, but the Missis did. 'We're ready for the camera now,' says she.

SPRUCED UP

Last week the men came to our place to take pictures of me and the Boss for the telly. This isn't to be the trial part, that comes later, over in England. When they came to the door, out walks the Boss, all smiles. His hair has hardly grown at all, and he was wearing a new Aran pullover, a check shirt and jeans. You'd have laughed if you could have seen the men's faces.

Before we started, one of them says, 'Now, Mr Kelly, wouldn't you like to change into your working clothes? You'd be much more comfortable, and it would give the viewers a better idea of your daily round.'

'Like hell,' says the Boss, very angry. 'What, be seen by millions in me working clothes? No way!' The man was very disappointed, but he couldn't force the Boss to change his clothes, so he had to make the best of it.

First, I was to bring the cows in, and the man was going to talk to the Boss while the cows stood about behind them. I was to go to the Boss and sit beside him looking reliable, and not leave him unless the cows wandered away. We have a new bull running with the cows. I can manage him easily, he's only a young one, but then, he never sees a stranger, let alone a pack of them with a red van and all their equipment.

The TV man says to the Boss, 'What about that bull? Is he quiet?'

'Oh, he's very gentle,' says the Boss. After that, things began to go wrong, I could tell.

The man knew the Boss only started trials this year, so he asks him his age. 'Sixty-two, what age are you?' snaps the Boss.

'I hardly think my age would interest the viewers,' says the man.

'Well, you can leave my age out of it as well,' says the Boss.

Just then, I stood up, because I saw the bull pawing the ground. 'Sit down, Shep,' says the Boss, very sharp because he was mad. I sat down, but I kept an eye on the bull. The next minute, he made a rush, straight at the famous telly man. I was too quick for him and I gave a spring and grabbed him by the nose. (I mean the bull's nose, not the man's.)

The bull ran away, the man mopped his face with his handkerchief and says, 'Blimey.'

The Boss says, 'Now you'll have some pictures worth seeing, so you will.' After that I rounded up the hens for the Missis.

SINGING ALONG

It's very hard for me to write about our visit to England. To start with, the journey is like a dream to me. The Missis put a St Christopher medal on me collar to keep me safe, and she gave me a pill called a 'Sea Leg', the way I wouldn't get sick on the boat. When I had the pill eaten I fell asleep and never budged till morning.

I was delighted when I saw the place where the trial was to be, because it was a real wild spot like the hilly place where Mr O'Brien used to train me. I had to run three times and I won every time. Everything went right for me from the start, the sheep were easy handled, and the Boss was whistling away without a care in the world. The Missis was so nervous she wasn't even able to watch.

When I had only one more run to do, the final, a newspaper man came over to the Boss.

'How does it feel to be about to run in the final?' says he.

'All right,' says the Boss.

'Are you nervous?'

'I am not,' says the Boss.

'Do you expect to win?'

'I might,' says the Boss, 'if I'm not pestered.'

'Oh dear,' says the man, 'I'm sorry; have a drink,' and he pulled a bottle of water out of his coat pocket – at least, it looked like water.

'What's that stuff?' says the Boss. 'Do you want to put

me drunk just when I need me wits about me?'

'Don't worry about that,' says the man, ''tis mother's milk; you could drink gallons of it.'

By this time, he had the top off the bottle, and the smell of what was inside would knock you kicking. The Boss seemed inclined to refuse, then he changed his mind and took a couple of decent swallows.

'You should give Shep some of that; it's powerful stuff,' says he. Then he went off to the start for the final.

He startled me a bit as we went out by giving a big shout, 'Up Coolcoffin! Galway for ever!' but after that he seemed fine and more sure of himself than I ever saw him. I wasn't at all surprised when I heard that we'd won. I was more than proud of meself, and as for the Boss, he was like a dog with two tails. He shook everyone in sight by the hand (even the Missis, by mistake) and had his photo taken over and over. Mine too. It's funny to think that two years ago he didn't know a shedding ring from a potting shed.

The newspaper man came back with another bottle of mother's milk. He'd been having some himself.

'Well done,' says he. 'Will you tell me something about your meteoric rise to stardom?'

'Could you ever leave off blethering, and talk decent English, the way a reasonable feller might make sense of you,' says the Boss.

After that, some of the lads that was running the show took us away in a car to go to a big dinner.

It was held in the biggest hotel in the town nearby, and all the men that ran dogs in the trial was invited.

The Boss was drinking pints in a pub with the other fellers for a while beforehand; then we all piled into cars and away with us to the dinner.

When we got to the hotel, the man at the door says, 'No dogs, please,' seeing me following the Boss. The Boss began to turn very red. 'No dogs!' says he. 'What do you mean, no dogs? If there weren't no dogs here, there wouldn't be no men either, or any dinner! Come on, Shep,' and with that he marched into the dining room, with me behind him.

I was the only dog there, so I lay quietly under the table, watching the Boss's new brown shoes and the Missis's red boots at the other side of the table, where she sat between a Welshman and a Scotsman.

It seemed a very dull meal to me. Of course, all I saw of the feed was a Brussels sprout the Boss dropped and I got that. The Boss was real happy that night, and when the Boss is happy he sings. I can sing too, and so can Jess. When we lived outside we used to sing on moonlit nights: 'How Much is that Doggie in the Window?', 'The Kerry Blues', all our favourite songs. We knew dozens. The Boss didn't like us to sing at night. If you heard his bedroom window open, it was time to stop. If you heard the back door open, it was too late.

When the Boss is happy, he sings a song called 'Spancil-hill'. It has forty-seven verses and he knows them all. The dinner was just finished when he started.

After fifteen or sixteen verses, I got a feeling the Missis was wanting him to stop and I thought maybe I could help. I'm a very healthy dog, so my nose is always cold and wet, and I pressed it against a bit of the Boss's leg that was showing between his trouser leg and the top of his sock. That was useless. All that happened was that the Boss roared out 'Lie down!' in between two verses and carried on. Then I thought, 'Well, if you can't beat 'em, join 'em,' so I sat up beside the Boss and pitched my voice carefully for the high note at the start of the nineteenth verse.

It was a bit wobbly, but dead on key, and very, very loud.

That did it; everyone clapped and laughed so loud the Boss had to stop. Then he made a speech and I went to sleep. They all had a great time, and me with nothing but one Brussels sprout inside me, after winning the old trial and all. It was after midnight before anyone thought of my supper.

DANGEROUS

It's grand to be home again after all me travels. I'd sooner the quiet life but the Boss is different. He always wanted fame.

When the Boss was young, a long time ago, he was a great man to play football, and even now he never misses a match if Coolcoffin is playing. Martin, who stayed at home to mind the place while we were in England, is a good footballer too, and the team and the supporters had a reception arranged for us.

The road from Dublin to Coolcoffin is long and con-tanglesome, so we came by train, and Martin met us in Coolcoffin with the car.

Now everyone who hasn't been to school knows that there's a bridge in the middle of Coolcoffin across the river. I know that river very well because I once nearly drowned in it trying to turn back some ducks. All Cool-coffin seemed to be waiting on the bridge and they were cheering and shouting.

The Boss was charmed. 'Well, upon me oath,' says he, 'we have a fine welcome home,' and he got out of the car with me. I hung back as the people crowded around because I was in dread they would walk on me feet. Then, before you could say 'Jock Richardson', the captain of the football team and his brother hoisted the Boss up on their shoulders – all sixteen stone of him – and carried him across the bridge. The Boss had a bad ride, because Patsy Fagan is over six feet tall and the brother is hardly as tall as the Missis. I thought he was going to finish up in the river and he thought so too, and started to roar out 'Let me go! Put me down!' and to use language I wouldn't like any pup of mine to hear.

I'm very fond of the Boss — mad about him in fact — I don't know why, and all of a sudden I forgot about not biting people, which is nearly as bad as biting a sheep at a trial, but not quite. I just wanted to see the Boss back on the ground, and so I did, though not just how I meant.

I ran forward and bit Patsy Fagan's ankle. He was wearing purple socks and tasted dreadful. It wasn't a real hard bite and I suppose you could say it worked. It isn't possible for anyone to stand on one leg for long with a sixteen-stone angry man sitting on his shoulder. Patsy Fagan tried to do it, and they all came crashing to the ground in a heap.

The worst of it was I wasn't quick enough to get away and that's why I'm all strapped up with three broken ribs. The Boss has a big lump on his head, and they tell me Patsy Fagan has blood poisoning.

Me Mammy told me when I was a little pup never to bite people and she was right. No good ever comes of it.

THINKING

You can't work with three broken ribs, so I was laid up for a while after we came back from England, and many's the hour I spent lying under the kitchen table.

Having time for thinking, I used to wonder how humans got some of their funny notions. What could be nicer than to be sold a pup? What better place to be than in the dog-house? What's wrong with going to the dogs? All those are bad things when humans say them. It isn't fair at all, so it's not. And whoever heard of anyone being dogged by good luck? It's always bad. I think it's time they talked about going to the cats for a change. Not that I've anything against cats as long as they sit still.

Sometimes the Missis would bring in one or two of the new pups. They were advertised for sale and most of them was sold.

One day, as I lay under the kitchen table pondering, a car came into our yard with a real well-dressed young woman driving it. The Missis was vexed because the Boss was away and she was busy baking. She cheered up when it turned out the woman was buying a pup, and they went off to choose one. Then they came in to draw the pup's markings and choose his name.

'I'll call him "Fluffy",' says the woman.

'I wonder would that be right,' says the Missis. 'When he's grown he'll be hairy.'

'Well, I can't call him "Hairy",' says the woman. 'Put down "Fluffy". I'm Miss D. Byrne, but do call me Deirdre, won't you? What beautiful bread! Do you always bake your own?'

Soon herself and the Missis was chattering like starlings and it came out that the Missis had made a stone of plum jam because the Boss likes it on new bread.

'He'd eat jam till it came out of his ears,' says the Missis. Then she says, 'Call me Kathleen,' and told Deirdre how she knitted Aran jumpers for the Boss because it was hard for him to fasten his shirt on account of being size nineteen.

'Fascinating,' says Deirdre. 'Do you know, Kathleen, I write a little column for a new woman's magazine called *Herself*. Would you allow me to put in a few words about your delicious bread and so on?'

'I don't mind,' says the Missis, 'but I don't see anyone wanting to read it.'

Sometime after, the postman brought a free copy of *Herself* for the Missis. When she had it read, she handed it to the Boss, real upset.

'I never told her to write all that,' says she.

'What's all this about?' says the Boss. '"Kathleen, who laughingly admits to more than half a century in this remote corner of Ireland, is a plump housewife with merry blue eyes. I was sorry not to meet the redoubtable Mr Kelly, the sheepdog enthusiast, who revels in Kathleen's cooking. Mr Kelly, who takes a majestic size nineteen in shirt collars, claims that his favourite food is Kathleen's fresh crusty soda bread, heaped with plum jam."'"

'She seemed so nice,' says the Missis, nearly crying. 'She asked me to call her Deirdre.'

'I'll call her Deirdre if I ever find her here,' shouts the Boss. 'Let two women start talking, and a man can't even call his neck his own! I'll sue her for libel! I'll see her in prison!'

I got up stiffly and walked out to the cowshed for a bit of peace.

WORRIED

It's a good while now since I got me ribs broke and I'm as good as new again. I was awful sore for a while, not able to work, or even to eat me dinner sometimes. Then I got woeful thin and me hair began to fall out. The Missis took me to the vet then, and he gave her some yellow tablets for me. 'Just melt these in warm water,' says he, 'and bathe the bare parts. He'll soon have a fine coat again.'

The Missis did as he told her, and she put the tablets she had over in a little bottle up on a shelf in case I'd get the same trouble again.

The Boss wasn't bothering himself much about me at that time, because himself and Martin was away fencing every day on an out-farm. I used to go with them in the car when I was getting better.

One day, the two of them was setting barbed wire on the top of a little narrow bank when the Boss caught his foot in a root and tumbled head, neck and heels into a big bog drain. He came out swearing and choking, black from his head to his feet, and blaming Martin for not catching him.

'Come on home,' says Martin. 'You'll catch your death.'

'I will not,' says the Boss. 'That's not the spirit that gets you onto the Irish team. We'll finish the job.'

When we got home, hours later, the Boss was shivering

44

and shaking, and he went straight in and got the whiskey bottle out of the press. Then he got my bottle of tablets off the high shelf.

'May as well take a few aspirins and be safe,' says he. He shook three or four of the tablets out of the bottle and downed them with the whiskey.

The Missis came in from the garden and saw him all bog mud half-dried, and she told him he should go to bed.

'I think I will,' says the Boss. 'I feel a kind of quare. Tell us, are those yellow aspirins any use?' The Missis grabbed the bottle with a screech that put the heart crossways in me.

'That's not aspirin,' says she. 'Look at the label! They're what I got from the vet, for Shep's skin trouble. They aren't to be eaten at all. They could be a deadly poison! Oh, what'll I do at all?'

Martin didn't wait to hear the rest. He was in the car and flying off for the doctor in Coolcoffin.

The Boss crept into bed just as he was. The Missis was crying and running to the door every few minutes to see was the doctor coming.

I got so worried I did what I never did before or after. I went up the stairs and had a look at the Boss inside in the bed. He was as yellow as the tablets, and what was worse, he didn't shout or tell me to go to hell. He just lay there groaning.

Then the doctor came and I hid under the bed. The Missis showed the doctor the yellow pills and he says, 'Well, you can set your minds at rest. Mr Kelly has a nasty chill, but these won't do anything worse than make him feel sick.'

The Boss sat up at once. 'Do you mean to say I'm not poisoned?' says he. 'Those old vets know nothing at all.' Then he gave a big shout. 'What's that damn dog doing up here? Get out of that!' I was delighted to see him more like himself, but I didn't wait to be told twice.

FAITHFUL

Wouldn't you think after all the stuff that was wrote about me and the Boss and the Missis that they'd have got enough of being famous and having their photos took for the paper and all?

One morning, the Boss came downstairs with his suit on, and the Missis with her hair curled up and those red boots. As soon as she had the dishes washed, she got my brush and set about me till my skin hurt. I knew there was something bad coming, and before long a young feller arrived in a big car. It turned out he was to take our pictures for the *Coolcoffin Courier*. For bad luck, the Boss was in a terrible humour. He cut his face shaving, trod on the cat and got his electric bill, all in about ten minutes. The poor ould divil, anyone would pity him. The Missis seemed nervous and shy with the young man. He wasn't shy. He called the Missis 'dear' and me 'Sheppie'. Me and the Boss hated him on sight.

'Would you like to see Shep working sheep?' asks the Boss.

'No, indeed,' says the young man, who was called Brendan. 'I want the two of you to stand in the doorway with old Sheppie here. Put your arm round Kathleen's

waist,' he says to the Boss, 'and see if Sheppie will sit beside you, looking up at you with his soul in his eyes.'

'Dogs have no souls,' says the Boss, 'it's been proved.'

'Looking up adoringly then,' says Brendan. I didn't like Brendan, so I looked at me feet and only squinted up sideways when the Boss spoke to me.

'Will I get him a bit of liver,' says the Missis, 'and hold it up for him?'

'No!' roars the Boss. 'Look at me, you villain!' This was to me, of course, and I did, but not adoringly and with me ears back. 'Click' went the camera.

I will say for Brendan he had great courage, for next he asked the Boss to sit on the step with one arm round me, and the big silver cup we won in the other hand. The Boss squatted down on one knee and grabbed me by the collar, while the Missis went to fetch the cup.

'Please take your pipe out of your mouth,' says Brendan, 'I can't see you for smoke.' The Missis came back with the cup and the Boss took a hold of it and put his pipe on the step in front of me. I shut me eyes and coughed.

'Big smile now, Mr Kelly,' says Brendan. The Boss bared his teeth. 'Click' went the camera again, and the Boss jumped up.

'That's enough,' says he, 'I'm off. Take a picture of the Missis if you want another; I have sheep to sort. Come on, Shep.'

When the *Coolcoffin Courier* came on Tuesday, the Boss looked at it and threw it on the floor. I came out from under the table and had a look. Right in the middle of the front page was a lovely picture of the Missis sitting on the doorstep with one arm round Tiny and the other round Jess, and her lap full of puppies. There was a small picture of me and the Boss at the side, but you couldn't call it good.

This week, the Boss bought the *Connacht Tribune*.

ALL SHOOK UP

They say a good dog keeps learning till he dies, and it's a fact. I learn all the time.

A dog at a trial once told me I led a sheltered life, and when I told him how the rain blows in under the henhouse when the wind is in the west, he nearly died laughing. That day, I learned to keep me mouth shut when I'm not sure of me subject.

Last week I learned something else. You have to have a licence to keep a dog but not a cat, and the Missis has to have one as well. I suppose you would call it a woman licence. I must find out.

It was a grand day, and Tiny, Jess and meself was sitting on the step in the sun. Jess has six pups, almost ready to go, and they were there too, having a right game with an old pullover belonging to the Boss. (He didn't miss it yet.)

Around dinner time, Guard Whelan rode into the yard on his bike. He wanted to buy some chickens off the Missis. He came to the door and couldn't get near it for dogs, so he tried to push me out of his way. Guard or no Guard, I wasn't having that, and I let a growl to warn him.

'He won't touch you at all,' says the Missis, opening the door.

'He'd better not,' says the Guard, keeping at the back

of his bike. 'How many dogs have you, altogether? Have you licences for them?'

'We have not,' says the Misiss, 'we never bothered getting them.'

'You'd better start bothering, unless you want a fine,' says Guard Whelan. 'I can manage not to see Shep as long as he doesn't growl at me, but there's nine dogs here. You'd better see to it at once.'

He sounded so vexed, me and Tiny thought the Missis needed protecting, and we went and stood one each side of her growling our best. (Jess is a pacifist.)

The Guard backed away in a hurry. 'Get those licences today,' says he. 'I'll be round again tomorrow – in the squad car.'

The Missis was in a terrible way. She was on her own because the Boss and Martin had gone to something called an open day with Jamesy Quinn. They left the car after them.

Now the Missis is getting driving lessons off and on from Martin for the past year. Martin is a bad teacher, and the Missis will never make an international driving champion, I'm afraid. She's very much in dread. All the same, she said she'd drive to Coolcoffin as it's a fair walk, and the post office might be closed on her. I got in the boot as usual.

It seemed a long time till we stopped, and then there was a lot of running forward and back in jerks like a bad dog at the pen. I didn't know then what was happening, but I found out later the Missis was having a hard time trying to back the car into a No Parking place between Colonel Crankshaft's Land-Rover and a Post Office van.

At last, there was a great crash and the sound of glass breaking, and the boot lid kind of bent in on me. I was too frightened to notice much, but I heard a crowd collecting, and felt the car rocking when they tried to open the boot.

They had to call the Fire Brigade to get me out, and

there were two Guards writing in books. Strange ones, from Galway.

'Where's your licence?' says one to the Missis.

'I haven't one,' says she, wiping her eyes. (She was crying because she thought I was killed stone dead inside in the boot.)

That was how I found out that the Boss has to have a licence to keep the Missis, just like us dogs. We had a bad few hours waiting for him to come home. The Missis made an apple cake to put him in good humour, but she was so shook up she let it burn.

It was late when the Boss came home. I ran out and licked his hand, while the Missis helped him take off his coat.

'What the hell is wrong with you all,' says he, 'and where's the car?'

When he heard what happened, he was so glad there was no one hurt he didn't say much at all. Besides, he'd won two tickets for the All-Ireland Hurling Final in a draw.

We all have licences now.

INJURED

That old book, *Breeding and Training Sheepdogs for Profit and Pleasure*, was wore out altogether with being read. The cover was loose, there was a page or two missing, and the Missis had dropped a fried egg on the chapter about 'Feeding and Hygiene' when she was giving it to the Boss and he jogged her elbow.

One day, the Boss saw an advert saying you could have a signed copy sent from England and he was after winning a few pounds on a bet, so he said he'd treat himself and he sent away for it. When it arrived the Boss could hardly wait to tear the paper off. 'I think this is the best book I ever read,' says he to the Missis, and he opened it to see what was wrote inside. Then there was a dead silence and I looked up to see what was wrong. The Boss was staring at the inside of the book with his mouth open.

'Well, that beats Banagher,' says he at last, in a strangled sort of voice.

'What's the matter?' says the Missis, anxiously. 'Did he forget to sign it or what?'

'Sign it, is it?' gasps the Boss. 'Oh yes, he signed it all right. He's a woman, so he is.'

'Come Bye, a woman? Are you sure?' asks the Missis.

'Of course I'm sure,' says the Boss. 'I never heard of a man called Gwendolen, did you? Gwendolen Rose Hopkins.' He got up and stamped out of the house.

The Missis picked the book up off the floor and put it on top of the dresser. It wasn't mentioned since.

I hardly have to tell you that the Boss was not in a good temper at dinner time the same day, so it was a pity that Martin had brought home a copy of the *Coolcoffin Courier* and there was a bit in it about the festival they're having soon.

The Boss began to read aloud. His face was very red and his voice shook: '"The Coolcoffin Festival Committee has decided to abandon the projected Sheepdog Trial in favour of a Dog Show, as the latter would have more spectator appeal. A further meeting will be held on Friday night."'

'It will that,' says the Boss, grinding his teeth, 'and I'll be there. Spectator appeal, be the holy!'

Of course, last year we had a trial and I won it and the Boss got a lovely statue. He was wanting another for the other end of the mantelpiece.

I didn't know what a committee meeting was but it sounded dangerous to me. I know now all right. What's more, I've even been to one and lived to tell the tale.

Nowadays, the Boss takes me with him nearly everywhere. Even so, I was surprised when he took me to the meeting of the Coolcoffin Festival Committee. It was held in the back room of Brophy's Bar and was very exciting. It's hard for me to explain what a committee is and what it does, so that other dogs can understand. Try to imagine a big field with about twenty sheep in it and an open pen in the middle of it. The chairman is the handler and he has to pen them. It's difficult for him because the sheep all come from different flocks and they run all ways, bleating away. Then, when they're penned, or most of them, the chairman has to make them stay inside when the gate is open and he has to persuade them that they like it there and that it was their own idea to go in. That's bad explaining, so it is, but I'm not able to do it any better.

The committee all had different notions about what events they would have on the Sunday afternoon.

'A sheepdog trial, what else,' says the Boss, loudly. Straight away, everyone began to talk at once. They said the field was wanted for a tug-of-war and a wellington-throwing competition. Then when the Boss said that Jim Dolan's little field would do for them, he was told there would be a beauty contest and a baby show going on there.

The Boss began to shout a bit, and soon they were all shouting. No one hit anyone else, though I was sure they would and I was all ready to go for anyone who attacked the Boss. At last, the chairman banged his pint of stout on the table as hard as he could without breaking the glass and most of the others stopped shouting to listen.

'As far as I can make out,' says the chairman, 'Jack Kelly is the only man here that wants a sheepdog trial, and he can always enter his dogs in the dog show. There's to be a class for Collies; they're all the go. And if they're good enough they might win some prizes.'

The Boss lepped up, nearly bursting with rage. In fact, he stepped on me tail with his tackety boot, which he wouldn't do if he was himself. I gave a loud yelp, but no one heard with all the racket going on.

The Boss says furiously, 'I never heard such a thing in all me life. I wouldn't be found dead in a dog show. You'll be telling me next to enter for the beauty contest!' At that, everyone began laughing, and the Boss made for the door. 'Come on, Shep, we're not wanted here,' says he. 'I resign.' He stamped out into the bar and bought himself a whiskey.

It wasn't long before the others came out and joined us. They all like the Boss and they persuaded him back onto the committee. He is to judge the wellington-throwing to make up for not having a sheepdog trial.

And he never even said he was sorry about me tail.

EXASPERATED

I suppose you must be wondering how Tiny is getting on with his training, but indeed he is not getting on at all; it's worse he's getting. The Boss could get no good of him, even though he was mad for work. They never hit it off, and the Missis was sick of Tiny as well, because he was forever slipping his collar, and when he did nothing was safe. The hens took to the trees and the cats too – if they had time. They sent Tiny away to Mr O'Brien's place in the Slievemoyne Hills to be trained.

Mr O'Brien brought him back himself, and I could tell he wasn't happy.

He says, 'Mind this fellow, won't you? He could be as good as Shep if you have patience.'

'Are you making out I'm short of patience?' asks the Boss threateningly. 'I expect to run him and Shep in braces this summer.'

Of course, every pup knows that a 'brace' is when two dogs run together, but the Missis says, 'Now Jack, you must keep your jacket on, or wear a belt. No one wants to see your braces.'

While they were all talking, Tiny slipped away and soon there was a great cackling and quacking from outside. The Boss and the Missis rushed out, and Mr O'Brien shook his head sadly.

'Poor Tiny,' says he.

That week the Boss really got down to working me and Tiny together. I used to say to Tiny, 'If you can't behave yourself you'll be sold, and then you'll be sorry.' Tiny didn't care. I think he really didn't hear the Boss roaring when he got excited, although I know it's hard to believe.

When the sheepdog trial for the festival was changed for a dog show and the Boss was so sore, they asked him would he give a demonstration with me. That would have been fine, but the Boss is very ambitious and he thought he'd put on a better show if he used Tiny too. Tiny is a great little dog to pen sheep, but the Boss doesn't dare let him go far away. I thought we would get away with it but it wasn't our lucky day.

The main event that day was a fancy-dress parade and the children were all getting ready to start in our field. One girl was Little Bo-Peep and she had a big pet lamb with her; as big as me he was. The Boss was doing most of his show with me for safety's sake, so he had his eye off Tiny when he spotted the lamb. Away went Tiny at top speed, and tried to fetch the lamb. I'm sure you know there's nothing in the world as hard to move as a pet lamb, so no harm was done there – they just faced one another. The bad trouble came when the Boss couldn't get Tiny back and had to go for him. Tiny dodged in and out among the children and wouldn't stop or come back. There was a big fat lad on a pony – he'd gone as Brian Boru. Tiny gave the pony a nip on the heel as he went by. The pony bucked, Brian Boru turned the wildcat and landed in some nettles. He was still roaring when we went away with the sheep.

The worst of it all was that the lad turned out to be a TD's nephew and his father was responsible for having a dog show instead of a sheepdog trial. He came down in a rage and accused the Boss of setting a dog on his son's pony out of spite. The Missis went down to her sister's house for the evening and I went back to me old place under the henhouse.

Martin has an entry in the song contest, but somehow I don't think he'll win.

UNDER THE WEATHER

I am a dull dog now, so I am. Everything is going agin me. For a start, me tail was damaged when the boss stepped on it at that meeting and I had to go to the vet and get injections. I've heard that the man that wrote one of the Boss's favourite books says he likes to see a dog with a dead tail. Mine was much better when it was alive.

Tiny was in big trouble over biting the Minister's nephew's pony at the Coolcoffin Festival, and he killed two hens since. That makes eleven since Christmas. I'd warned him many a time and I was right. The Boss made up his mind to sell him.

That week he advertised Tiny in the *Farmers' Journal* and I don't know how many people came to see him. Sometimes when they came, Tiny had got loose and gone for a walk. Other times, he would be giving them a right show and he'd spoil it by going out of the field and bringing in Jamesy Quinn's bullocks through the ditch or something like that. I don't think anyone got as far as asking the price.

At last the Boss decided to take Tiny to a dog sale. I went too, looking like a right eejit with the end of me tail in a splint. I wasn't supposed to go, but I love riding in the car boot now, so I thought I'd go for the spin. I jumped in with Tiny, and the Boss didn't bother to turn me out.

The sale was good for good dogs, but Tiny wasn't

being a good dog that day. Him and the Boss had to give a show with some sheep, and Tiny went round them like an aeroplane. The Boss was dizzy from turning round and round. Tiny had the sheep packed around him as tight as murder so he couldn't push his way through them. I was watching with the Missis and he had to shout for me to come and help.

After the show, the dogs was sold by auction and no one wanted Tiny. I don't blame them – he takes after his mother's side of the family.

When it was all over, the Boss was going back to the car when a small little man with broken teeth came over and asked how much for Tiny. I didn't like the look of him at all. Inbred and badly reared, I thought, and could do with a dose.

He said he was called Chris something-or-other. The Boss asked £150 and Chris says with a nasty laugh, 'I'll give you £50. I don't want him at all except to tame him and maybe make a few pounds.'

Our old friend, Mr O'Brien, was standing near and he nudged the Boss with his elbow and says, 'Don't be in a hurry to sell, Jack. He'll make a top-class dog yet.' Chris went off and Mr O'Brien says, 'Watch that boyo. I know him well; his cheque could bounce.'

The Boss says, 'Thanks, but I have no other man for Tiny today.'

'You're better off with no one than Chris,' says Mr O'Brien. 'He's bad news and I should know: he lives near me. Anyway, I wouldn't take a bad price for Tiny; he'll make a great cattle dog.'

'I know that,' says the Boss. 'Show him bullocks and he'll bring them, dead or alive.'

While we were going home that evening, Tiny ate all the wires in the boot, so the back lights went out and the Boss got a summons. It was a lucky thing Chris didn't come this way since, as he'd have got a present of Tiny; that's one thing sure and certain.

NOT IMPRESSED

Tiny isn't to be sold after all. The Boss has his mind changed again. He says now that there isn't enough money in Ireland to buy him.

You wouldn't have thought that two days ago. Tiny chased our big ginger tom cat and cornered him at the back door. The Missis heard the spitting and growling outside, so she opened the door and Ginger rushed into the kitchen and up on the dresser, where he broke five plates and a milk jug. Tiny, who had been working cattle in the back yard and was rather dirty, couldn't get up on the dresser, so he jumped onto the kitchen table, which was half-way there. It was set for the dinner.

When the Boss came in, he says, 'That's it. I'm going to shoot Tiny.'

'No, no,' says the Missis. 'Take him to the vet or the cruelty man; it's kinder.'

They argued all through dinner. Either way, things looked black for Tiny. I went out and sat in the cowshed with Jess, who is Tiny's mother, feeling very low.

After the dinner, the Boss came out with a dog chain in his hand and went into Tiny's shed. I heard him shout to the Missis.

'Did you let Tiny loose? He's gone.' It was the same old story, of course; Tiny had slipped his collar. I don't know how he does it – I couldn't.

They both looked for him all over (the Missis didn't look very hard). Then Martin came in and took the two of them off to see the opening of the new hall. I went with them in the boot, as I usually do. I thought it might be interesting, and perhaps it was. They may have opened the new hall, but no one opened the boot, so I don't know. When we got home, Martin let me out, and we went off for the cows. There was a young bull with them and we used to bring him in too. He was never any bother since the time when he went for the high-up telly man and I had to stop him.

There was mushrooms in the field, and the Missis gave Martin a bag, and asked him to bring some for the tea.

When we got to the field we heard crying and scream-ing, and there was two little lads with a mushroom basket, trying to get through the blackthorn ditch. The bull was standing, blowing, with his head down, and Tiny was flying in at him, nipping his nose and barking. I galloped to join him, and between us we hunted the bull right away. Martin took the little lads back home to the next farm, and then with his help we got the bull into a stable.

He went away yesterday in a lorry. I think maybe he went to be put to sleep by the cruelty man instead of Tiny. Tiny is in a right mess – he got tossed and walked on. He's all cuts and bruises, and today he can hardly move.

The Missis brought him in last night, crying buckets over what didn't happen, and she washed him all over with my special soap. Of course, he got away and ran into the best room and shook himself and rolled on the mat. Then he sat down as bold as brass on the settee, and nobody cared at all.

I am not top dog any more.

PILL POPPIN'

Now that Tiny isn't to be sold, the Boss is talking about selling Jess. What's worse, Jess has no chance of saving herself by facing a bull because she is a union dog and only works when she feels like it, which is hardly ever. The Missis doesn't want to sell her because twice a year she has five or six pups, and she's great to mind them. Tiny is the only one that didn't get sold, and that was because he was always missing when there were customers around.

Another thing about Jess, she has real beauty. I know humans think they are good-looking themselves. Martin has a girlfriend called Julia; he's going to marry her when he gets time, and he thinks she's beautiful, the poor harmless man. Of course I could be prejudiced about this, not being the bare-skinned type meself, but wait till you hear about Jess. She has lovely eyes; one is a deep brown and the other, the right one, is a kind of milky white. You never saw anything like that on a woman, did you? I thought not.

The only thing that could save Jess from getting sold is that it might be hard to find anyone to buy her. Let's hope so. I prefer her company to Tiny's except when she's rearing pups. The Boss has no interest in pups and that makes two of us – neither have I. When Jess says 'Which one do you like best?' I say they're all lovely and try not to look at the nasty, little, blind things. She'd bite me if I looked too close anyway.

When the Missis dosed the first litter of pups for worms, she lost count and dosed Bess twice and missed Tiny. I think that's why Tiny stayed so small. It didn't do Bess any good either. There's an ad on the telly for a worm dose called Vermolin. A reliable-looking man is holding up a bottle while someone sings, 'The Vermolin goes in, the worms come out and that's what it's all about.'

The Missis came down the yard one day with a strange man. She had a bottle of Vermolin in her hand and she gave some to all of us, even me. I didn't know what she was up to, or I'd have spat it out. Then the man took my photo.

Some time later, one evening, the Missis says to me, 'Look, Shep, you're on TV again.' I looked and the Vermolin man was on. Then a picture of me came up and a voice says, '"I'm free of parasites now," says Shep, "thanks to Vermolin!"'

What a thing to do to me! I never said anything about the stuff. I might be full of parasites, whatever they are, for all I know, and the old dose tasted worse than Patsy Fagan's purple socks the day I bit him on Coolcoffin Bridge. What's more, I hear they got money for it. I hate to think what my friends at the trials will say. I'll never hear the end of it.

There's one comfort. I think the Boss is on my side about this. I noticed he had nothing to do with it.

DISGUSTED

At the pub, the Boss drinks stout, which isn't too bad if you're thirsty, but when he's at a special do he drinks whiskey. Whiskey smells desperate and tastes worse. (They're always slopping it around, although they make out it's dear.)

The kind of whiskey the Boss likes best is called Black Dog. It is made in our own county. A second cousin of the Boss is working for the main man's wife's sister, so naturally they went to the Boss when they were going to bring out a new kind of whiskey.

This new whiskey was to be called Hair of the Dog, which is a foolish name if you ask me.

Not being interested I didn't bother me head when I heard the Boss and the Missis going on about the whiskey, until I heard me own name mentioned. I think whiskey beats the Devil out. I don't know how they drink it. It hardly seems right for me to advertise the stuff, but my picture was to be on the labels. I don't know at all why that would make anyone buy it. There was to be a big party for it in Galway, called a launching. (I thought that was boats. Wrong again.)

The Missis loves a party and she was off to Galway and came back with a long black dress.

'You should have a dress suit, Jack,' says she to the Boss. 'They're to be had for hiring.'

'You want to make a laughing-stock of me,' says the Boss, and he put on his blue suit and his grey pullover. I thought he looked great, but the Missis fussed about, not satisfied at all.

'Now don't drink too much of that stuff,' says she. 'I'm not driving home.' (She has driving given up.) 'And mind and call me Kathleen or I'll kill you.'

'All right, so,' says the Boss. As a rule he calls her Mam, but her registered name is Kathleen. Mam is her working name.

It must have been the kind of launching I know about, because I heard you could swim in the whiskey. (Ugh!) I didn't go. I stayed with Jess who has the pledge taken.

'It's all right for the Boss,' says she. 'It's innocent bitches and puppies that suffer.'

'Nobody suffers here when the Boss takes too much except the Missis,' says I. I have to stand up for the poor feller.

The man who makes the whiskey is called Mr Flanagan. The Boss came home singing a song about

The whiskey that's brewed by Tim Flanagan,
Drink it all up, be a man again.
Fill up as fast as you can again...

I heard him at it for a long time. I think it's very unfair that we are not allowed to sing at night.

The next day, I was listening to the two of them talking at the dinner, and they had me puzzled.

'What's "sponsored", do you know?' says I to Jess.

'It's either chained up very tight, or else it's some class of an operation,' says Jess, who knows most things.

I'm wondering why the Boss is so pleased. Him and me is supposed to be going to be sponsored by this Mr Flanagan. I suppose Jess could be wrong. I hope so.

This evening the Boss says to me, 'You're getting a new name, Shep, but I'm damned if I'll use it.' I found out since what it is. I heard the Missis talking about it.

Flanagan's Flockmaster. Me. The cheek of them.

SUCCESSFUL

I'm not Flanagan's Flockmaster any more. I'm back to Shep and glad of it. It seems that the Sheepdog Society that we all belong to won't let us be sponsored at all. I'm glad of it; I didn't like the sound of it. There is to be a black greyhound on the whiskey labels, and the Boss was raging mad.

He's not mad any more, because we got onto the Irish team for the International Trial, and that's what he's been wanting to do ever since that trial at Oughterard. It was his heart's desire, he said, and now he's managed it.

To get on the team, we had to be in the first eight in the Irish National Trial, up in Donegal. The Boss got a lift with his friend Jim Dolan, who owns a dog called Ben who won a few trials. Jim Dolan is a big heavy man with a beard, who likes a song and likes a pint. He sings in a group called Irish Stew. He has a car called a stationary wagon with a glass back on it and no boot, so we could see out.

Ben and me had a fine time looking out at the other dogs having to walk, and listening to the Boss and Jim arguing. First they argued about hurling, then it was barley, then greyhounds. Soon they were arguing about trials.

'The best sheep for trials is Suffolks,' says the Boss.

'Cheviots is better, and Scotch Hornies is best of all,' says Jim.

'They are not,' says the Boss. 'They're useless. Texels, now, is a bit stubborn.'

'The Scotch Mountainy sheep is way the best,' says Jim.

'They might be all right for a weak dog,' says the Boss.

Before long, the two of them got very angry altogether. They shouted away, and Jim was so vexed he was driving like a bat out of hell. 'Heavy sheep is no good only for a slow old dog,' says he.

'There's no need to shout,' says the Boss. 'I have me hearing, thanks be to God.'

We went round a corner so quick, Ben let a yelp out of him, and Jim twisted round to tell him to be quiet. He made a mistake looking round like that. There was another old bend in the road, and the car ran straight into a big bank. By the grace of God the two of them had seat belts on them or they'd have been killed dead. Ben and me had no seat belts. Ben landed on Jim's lap and I landed on the Boss's.

We were all so shook, we just sat there. In a few minutes who should come along only Mr O'Brien in his big car. So he stopped and we left the stationary wagon after us and went on with him.

They used light Mountainy sheep at the trial, and Jim and Ben made no hand of them at all. The Boss and me like heavier sheep. We didn't think we'd finish the course. It was something like the time when the Boss had new teeth and couldn't whistle. I won then. This time it was shock that kept him fairly quiet, and things went well for us. We came fifth, and got onto the team.

There was a second day and we stayed over. The Boss and Jim met friends and one way and another we didn't land home until Sunday.

Jim's car had been taken from the road where he left it. He thought it wouldn't go, but it did. Two lads took it and the Guards found it in Waterford, in bits.

We had to go home in a bus and Ben got sick. It's the diesel goes against him, he says. The Boss said that under-bred dogs are often poor travellers, and after that him and Jim sat at the two opposite ends of the bus. They didn't talk since.

The International Trial is to be in Wales. The Missis and Martin is coming, and all Coolcoffin in a coach.

'Shep and me will uphold the honour of Ireland,' says the Boss.

I hope I don't let him down.

CLAIRVOYANT

The International Trial has been and gone, and I thought we'd win it. I really did. The disappointment is terrible. When he got home the Boss stayed in bed for three days, and the Missis cried.

It's a funny thing about people, but as far as I know, they're not able to see ghosts. I never saw the ghost of a man until I went to Wales, but I saw the ghosts of plenty of dogs in my time. They do no harm. I've often wondered could sheep see ghosts. I know now that they can.

A whole crowd of us went over to Wales. I'm well used to travelling now, so there wasn't a bother on me. The Boss told everybody we'd win, and he was mad because they didn't pay any heed to him.

The Trial went on for three days, and I had to run on the first day. On the last day, the best fifteen would run again over a bigger course for the final. There was a dresser-load of prizes for the winner, and the Boss was wondering how would he manage in the customs when our number was called.

There were five sheep and I went off to fetch them as cool as you like. I never felt better, and I knew I was doing great. I had the best outrun of the day. I used to think an outrun was what the cat did when the Missis caught him in the kitchen. Live and learn.

The next thing is the lift. Now that's a funny thing as

well. You don't lift anything – not that you could. It means turning in on the sheep at the end of the field. It was my day. The further I went, the better I went, until I came to the pen. In the big trials, the pen isn't the last thing. You have to single out a sheep with a red collar afterwards. I wasn't worrying about that at all.

The Boss was mesmerised by the way things were going. I thought he was going to stay standing in the shedding ring and forget to open the pen for me. At the last moment he got moving, and came panting up to open the gate. There's six feet of rope on the gate and he had to hold the end of it. The sheep were just right, lined up ready to go in, when they all stopped in a slap.

I couldn't see what was stopping them, and I kept trying to move them until I saw that they'd break away if I kept on. I stopped and sat down, waiting for the Boss to say something. He did. 'Get up, you idle villain, go on out of that!' was what he said. So I went on and the sheep all wheeled away and I had to go and bring them back. As I got them lined up again, I saw what was wrong. There was a black and white dog with one eye sitting in the pen.

'What would you be doing there?' says I.

'Sitting down, amusing meself,' says the dog. He was from Scotland by his brogue.

'Well, get out,' says I. 'You're spoiling my Boss's run.'

The dog didn't move, and it was then I noticed I could see the bars of the pen through him.

'I was called Roy,' says he. 'I won three internationals

when your Boss was a pup. It's fifty years to the minute since I won me first, so I thought I'd put in an appearance.'

'You can disappear again as soon as you like,' says I. I knew I couldn't fight him. With that, the dog disappeared, and it was given out that we'd run out of time. As the Boss stamped off the field with me, I heard a whistle and I saw the one-eyed dog going off with a thin man in a cap.

'The Devil was in those sheep,' says the Boss to Martin when we got back.

'By the way they were acting, the Devil was in the pen,' says Martin.

Aren't they very unfortunate to be so blind?

DOG TIRED

The Boss has an idea that, the further you go to buy a dog, the better he'll be. This isn't always right. He sent to Wicklow for me and to Donegal for Jess, and then he found out that his friend Jim Dolan bred Jess's Mammy and sold her to go to Donegal to a man who had the same idea as the Boss.

The Boss thought it would be a right idea to buy a dog in Wales when we were over for the International, and Jim Dolan thought the same.

The Boss couldn't face going back with the crowd after the Trial. He had so much boasting done, the lads would've teased the life out of him. So Martin and the Missis went home, and me and the Boss stayed on along of Jim Dolan, to buy two dogs.

The International was spoiled for us by the ghost, but a Scottish dog told me I had seen J.M. Wilson and Roy, and that I should feel honoured. I tried to see it his way.

We saw the final and then the others went home and me and the Boss and Jim and Ben stayed on at a guest-house. Jim had brought Ben to Wales with him because he has no one to leave him with. He howls night and day when he is left, and sometimes he bites people when he forgets. Jim has a sister and he thinks she should mind him, but she won't.

The stationary wagon was smashed up altogether, and

Jim couldn't afford another, so he has a small little red Mini. He still drives like the wheels of hell. There is no boot in the Mini that you could put a dog in, so we sat in the back seat.

We were to go home on the Monday afternoon from Holyhead on the boat, so we had all Sunday and half Monday.

The Boss had met a man called Cymro at the trial, and he knew a farmer with a whole pile of dogs.

'He doesn't know the value of them,' says Cymro.

We drove a long way to see the dogs. 'What's the name of this place?' says the Boss.

'Ysgol,' says Jim, 'look at it on that sign.'

'G'way,' says the Boss. 'We came through Ysgol an hour ago. I noticed the name. Funny old names they have in Wales – nothing simple like Coolcoffin.'

'Are you sure about Ysgol?' says Jim.

'Of course I'm sure, you're driving round in rings,' says the Boss.

Jim stopped very sudden, and we drove back the way we came at seventy miles an hour. We soon got back to another town, and Jim stopped again. 'Ysgol. Look, will you?' says he.

'Is all the towns in Wales called Ysgol?' says the Boss to a little lad in the road. 'He says it's Welsh for a school. Whip her round, Jim; we were right before.'

Jim whipped her round, and back we went. After another hour or so we found the farm on a hillside. The man there had a pile of dogs all right. He had over twenty; all barking and running around. We stayed in the car while the Boss and Jim went off to see them work. When they came back, they were chatting away with the owner. They went into the house, and stayed until dark.

Much later, a woman came out and saw us. She went back to ask where would we be put for the night. Ben was howling.

Out came the Boss then and Jim. Jim had drink taken, and the Boss had had a small sup too. They put us in a stable, and we were fed. I ate Ben's food, he felt sick.

The Welsh dogs barked all night, and we could hear the Boss and Jim singing 'Spancilhill' in the house. Ben howled like a banshee, and I slept badly.

I thought I was still having nightmares next day. The Boss and Jim had bought four dogs.

RILED

I was glad to hear that the four dogs were all for Jim and a friend of his.

We were a tight fit in the Mini. I sat in front at the Boss's feet and the other five sat in the back.

The nearest dog to me was big and black. 'I'll introduce us,' says he. 'This is Taff, those two are Gwen and Meg. You may call me Bach.'

'Bark?' says I. 'I heard you last night.'

'Not Bark, Bach,' says the dog. 'I suppose you're Pat or Mick.'

'I'm Shep,' says I. 'I won on the telly.'

'I remember now,' says Bark. 'I thought Ifor Jenkins was in terrible hard luck.'

'I don't know about hard luck,' says I. 'His dog didn't take his commands when he was shedding.'

'How do you know? Do you know Welsh?' Bark was growling.

'I feel sick,' says Ben.

'I know you can't whistle in Welsh,' says I.

'Ah, shut up,' says Bark. 'Your Boss was drunk, anyway.'

There's limits to what I can stand, so I squithered through beside the seat and grabbed him by the neck. Taff came to help Bark, there was no room at all.

'Help me, Ben,' says I, with me mouth full of Welsh

wool.

'I'm going to be sick,' says Ben, and he was. Gwen and Meg, who weren't used to driving, were sick as well. They'd had meat dinners and milk.

'Stop, can't you,' roars the Boss. 'Jim, stop the car!'

'I can't,' says Jim, 'we'll miss the boat.' All this time, he'd been going down the narrow roads like a bullet.

The Boss opened his seat belt and twisted around. He knelt on the seat and beat us all with a rolled-up paper. It didn't hurt.

'For God's sake, stop,' says he. 'The Welsh Guards is after us.'

'They have policemen over here, not Guards,' says Jim, with his foot on the pedal. 'They won't touch us because we're tourists.'

'I wouldn't bank on it,' says the Boss. 'They're passing us out.'

I was still underneath Taff and Bark, so I couldn't see what happened.

I felt the car stop with a jolt, and all six of us fell in a heap with me at the bottom of it. I heard a strange voice say, 'Do you realise you were travelling at seventy-seven miles an hour?'

'Is that so?' says Jim. 'Your roads are so good, you wouldn't notice the speed creeping up on you.'

'You'll have to pay a fine.'

'I'll miss the boat to Ireland,' says Jim.

'Who owns all the dogs?' says the voice.

'He does,' says Jim and the Boss together.

'You aren't wearing your seat belt,' says the voice to the Boss.

'Have sense, man,' says the Boss. 'Would you, if there was three dogs fighting just behind you and three gettng sick?'

'You'll be hearing from us,' says the voice.

Soon we were off again as fast as ever, and never stopped until we reached a river with a notice, 'PRIVATE. NO BATHING.' Jim and the Boss took each of us in turn and washed us in the river. I was last out.

'Did you ever get washed before, since your Mammy washed you?' says Bark. I had to attack him again and Taff joined in and Ben, who was feeling better. Jim came to separate us and slipped, and me and him and Bark all fell into the river, so Jim got a wash as well.

A few carloads of people drove by, and they were all watching us. You'd think they never saw a dogfight before. Gwen got loose and was nearly run over. It was almost an hour before we were back on the road again.

SMELLY

Oh, it's great to be finished with travelling for a while. After we all got washed in the river, Jim drove faster than ever. We flew down the roads with the wheels bouncing on the bumps. I was sure we'd be over the ditch. We went through Holyhead as if we were going to a fire, and when we reached the harbour, there was the boat, the width of a small field out from the side, steaming away to Dublin without us. I did truly think Jim was going to drive into the sea after it. He stopped just in time, and him and the Boss had a right row.

They asked when was the next boat and were told it had gone, but there was one out of Fishguard in three hours.

'Fishguard? Where's that?' says the Boss.

'It's to the south,' says Jim. Down went the foot on the pedal, and we set off for Fishguard. By that time Bark, Taff and me was feeling sick, and Ben, Gwen and Meg thought they were dying. It seems it's further to Fishguard than Jim thought, and he lost his way twice. As well as that, we were stopped by the same policemen as before, and they took Jim's name.

It was the same old story. We landed into Fishguard as the boat left.

'That's it,' says the Boss. 'I'll travel no further with you. I'll walk sooner.' Him and me went to a place to stay until morning when there'd be another boat. We weren't there long when Jim arrived, begging the Boss to go with him to a place called Pembroke, where he'd get another boat. It seemed that when the Boss wasn't there, he couldn't keep the other five dogs out of the front seat. He was inclined to think it might be a bit dangerous.

The Boss is good-hearted if he's taken right, and we were soon on the road again. It was night, and a hard road to find, so Jim eased up a little and none of us was sick.

Pembroke at three in the morning isn't a great spot. I suppose it's not fair to judge it. Maybe a Welsh dog would think nothing of Coolcoffin at three in the morning.

We had five hours to wait. We all slept in the car. It was nice and warm, but you'd call it smelly if you were fussy.

Jim and the Boss were snoring away when it was time for the boat to go, so it was a good thing somebody woke them up.

Soon we were on the boat, and Jim says, 'Well, Jack, we're clear of Wales at last. Next stop Ireland.' While he was speaking, two policemen came in, and spoke to him by name.

'You've been reported,' says they. 'Overcrowding a car, beating six dogs while travelling at an excessive speed, no seat belt, attempting to drown two dogs, bathing in a private place and allowing a dog to stray onto the public highway.'

'It's your car, you go,' says the Boss.

So Jim went off with the policemen and the boat was delayed an hour and a half while they asked him questions. I don't know what happened, as Ben and me stayed with the Boss and the other dogs were in the car. The policemen seemed quite happy when they brought Jim back. One of them shook the Boss by the hand and the other patted Ben's head. By the grace of God, Ben didn't forget himself and bite him. He's handy with his teeth and he was feeling sick.

There was a big gale on the way back to Ireland. I thought we were going to Dublin, but no, it was Wexford, where the Boss once took me by mistake. Jim was desperate to get home and wouldn't delay a minute, so we set off at once on the long road right across Ireland.

Now he's home, the Boss says he'll never cross the water again, not for a hundred internationals. The Missis and Martin had a great time, but he doesn't want to hear about it.

FAMOUS

The parade in Dublin on St Patrick's Day is bigger than the one in Coolcoffin, but it isn't as good. Everyone around here says so. I never saw either of them meself until this year.

It was decided early on that me and the Boss was to be in it, right behind the band. The Coolcoffin Pipe Band is a new thing. It was started last year, and they played up and down the street. Me and Jess could hear them from the farm, and we joined in because it pained our ears. I didn't want to be just behind them at all. The Boss was looking forward to it.

When St Patrick's Day came, we had trouble on the farm. The Boss was rushing the milking along and telling Martin to hurry. He hurried too much himself, slipped on the flagstones outside the door, and measured his length on the ground. The Missis came flying out to help him up and he was groaning. 'Me leg is busted,' says he.

Martin went for the doctor and he said the leg wasn't busted at all, only bruised, but the Boss had his ankle sprained and he wasn't to walk.

'What about the parade today?' says the Boss.

'You'll have to ride on one of the floats,' says the doctor. So Martin drove us down to where the people was collecting.

Nobody wanted me and the Boss on their trailer. They

seemed to think it would spoil the design. We asked everyone.

The very last one we went to was the travel agency. They had a few girls in bathing-suits; palm trees and things like that.

The travel agent is the Boss's second cousin, so he had to say yes. He brought a chair out of the kitchen and put it up on the trailer. Then the Boss was hoisted up and I jumped up after him.

'Will you take that raincoat off you, Jack,' says the travel agent. 'You're spoiling me image.'

'I will not,' says the Boss.

We rode through the town in fine style. I was very proud. The Boss waved to everyone, but there was a small crowd. Most people were in the parade themselves.

When it was over, two Americans got to talking to the Boss and asking questions about me. They were full of old chat and gave us a lift home in their car.

'Would you like a part in a picture?' says one of them to the Boss.

'I would so,' says the Boss. 'I like a good cowboy meself.'

'This is a historic picture,' says the American. 'We want an old shepherd for atmosphere. You wouldn't have much to say, but you'd have to grow a beard.'

'I'm not growing any beard,' says the Boss.

'Never mind. If you can't grow one, we'll get Mr Denis O'Brien or Mr Jim Dolan,' says the feller. 'They could grow beards.'

'Who says I couldn't grow one?' says the Boss. 'I could grow one down to me knees if I wanted to.'

So now he's not looking like himself at all. The beard isn't coming along too badly, I suppose, but I don't think it suits him at all. The Missis has a job to keep from laughing when she looks at him.

'It's all in a good cause,' says the Boss.

Ever since he caught the trial bug last year, he's a changed man. I can't imagine him an actor even now. He has a part to learn. 'Lie down, Bob,' he has to say. (Bob is me.) Then he has to say, 'It looks like snow.' He has it all learned off already. My part is much harder. I have to howl on somebody's grave. They wondered how would they manage that until the Boss got a fine idea. We'll have the Coolcoffin Pipe Band playing behind the hedge.

'SNIGGER'

Coolcoffin is a sad place now. We are not to be film stars. And the Missis had it all made up how we were going on a cruise. I don't mind about that, I did enough cruising coming home from Wales.

The Boss got a letter after he'd been growing his beard for weeks and had told everyone why. He went off to the post office in the Devil's own temper and rang up the Americans, wanting to know why we weren't to be in the picture.

They told him they'd found a man with a bigger beard and a dog that would howl without an orchestra to accompany him. That wasn't fair. The Pipe Band wouldn't help, so Martin was going to play a few screeches on his fiddle instead. That would put me howling for ten minutes.

The Boss took it so hard, the American men called to see him. They told him they were real sorry and they'd let him know if there was something else.

'Who is this actor you've found?' the Boss wanted to know.

'Mr Jim Dolan,' says they. 'His dog is called Ben.'

After that, the Missis made a cup of tea and the Boss went upstairs and attacked his beard. The Missis didn't pay much heed to him. She let him get over it and said nothing. She manages better, I think, since she got liberated.

This liberation was a great thing. I never knew the Missis to be tied up, or locked in a room, so I was wondering how would anyone liberate her. She told the Boss about it and he said it was codology but she went to a meeting and came back liberated.

I couldn't see any difference meself, but some of the women is gone mad altogether. They're joining the hurling team and burning their vests. I think that's what the Missis said.

To go back to this old picture. A lot of people we knew were going to be in a crowd scene, but the Boss said he wouldn't stoop to act in a crowd, not when he'd nearly been a shepherd for atmosphere.

We don't keep many sheep here, only twenty ewes and a few wethers that are supposed to be getting fat. The Boss is always after them with us dogs, so they aren't getting fat very fast. In the spring, the Boss shears them with a machine yoked up to the electricity, and Martin wraps up the fleeces and clips off the dirty bits with the hand shears.

This day, the Boss was shearing away with the machine when the two Americans came back, and brought their cameras with them.

'What luck!' says they. 'Shearing time! Could you clip a sheep with the hand shears, and we'll put it in the picture.'

The Boss was sorry his beard was gone. He caught a sheep and began snipping away. The shears was a bit blunt, and it's not a thing he'd ever done. I was more than sorry for that sheep. The Boss didn't cut it often, but he was as slow as he could be. When it was nearly finished, it got away and Martin fell over me as we both tried to stop it. It had wool trailing from it, and it wasn't going to be caught again if it could help it.

Round and round the shed we went, and at last me and Martin and the Boss all dived at the sheep at once. It gave a big lep and landed straight on top of the camera. Its legs got tangled up in some wire somehow, and it and the two men rolled around on the ground. I thought it was very funny, but then I'm not well educated or anything.

The Boss isn't going to be shearing sheep in the picture.

DISMAYED

The Boss first met the Missis in a place called Lisdoon-varna in County Clare. Ever since, the two of them have taken a holiday there every September. Last September we were away at the International, so they decided they'd go to Lisdoonvarna for a weekend a bit later on.

When they go away, Martin and meself is left in charge of the farm. I draw the line at working for Martin. I might help him out if he was in trouble, but that's all. So Martin used to leave me lying in the sun on the doorstep when he went for the cows.

The Boss and the Missis left on the Friday morning, and the Missis left a dinner prepared for Martin. He was inside eating it when I heard a car tearing down the road; then I heard brakes and tyres squealing. Jim Dolan in his Mini came racing into the yard and flattened one hen. In the back of the car sat Ben, Taff and Bark.

Martin came out and peeled the hen off the cement. 'She'll make soup,' says Jim. He'd got wind of the Boss and the Missis going to Lisdoonvarna.

'I took the notion of going meself,' says he. 'I might meet a nice girl like your dad did.'

'They're gone since morning,' says Martin.

'I'll be there as soon as them,' says Jim. 'This is a great little car. Look, Martin, will you be a good lad and mind these dogs for me until Monday? You won't know you have them.'

'I have dogs enough to mind,' says Martin. 'I have three, and Ben bites people.'

'Not like he did,' says Jim. 'Not as hard nor as often.'

'I don't care,' says Martin. 'I won't have him here.'

Jim wasn't so pleased, but there was nothing he could do, and he had to take Ben with him.

'You can bring your cows in with Taff and Bark,' says Jim. 'They're millers to work.' Martin said nothing. He took Taff and Bark and shut them in the pony's stable.

'Good man, I'm grateful to you,' says Jim, getting into the car. 'If anyone comes this way with three hundred pounds in his pocket, you can sell him Bark. He is a little bit hasty with sheep.' With that, gravel flew all over as he roared out of the yard.

Taff is a harmless enough dog, a good worker and no trouble on his own. It's Bark is the bad influence. He is a big, long-legged, long-haired dog, with ears that stand

out sideways and wild, yellow eyes. I once heard Jim tell the Boss he never let him off the chain except to work, and I soon found out why. The bottom of the stable door was mended to keep Tiny in not so long ago. It is new timber and, before me very eyes, Bark tore it asunder. He pulled out boards a foot long with two-inch nails in them. He was out in a couple of minutes, and Taff after him.

Martin had gone back to his dinner. I says to Bark, 'Now look what you're after doing. Your Boss will have to pay for a new door.'

'He'll do no such thing,' says Bark. I did your Boss a favour there. That door was rotten, ready to fall apart. Now. Where do you keep your sheep? The trouble with Ireland is there's nothing to do.

'The sheep are sold,' says I. (That was a lie, may I be forgiven.) 'If you want a job, why don't you bring the bullocks up from the bog?'

That'll beat him, I thought, and I went back to the step. Taff, who doesn't like working cattle, came with me.

Five minutes later, all twenty bullocks ran bawling through the yard with Bark snapping at their heels. They broke down the gate and galloped into the Missis' vegetable garden. Me and Taff and Jess went under the henhouse. We wished the Boss was home.

SUSPICIOUS

Martin made a terrible mistake over Bark. This is what happened. The Missis grows all kinds of vegetables in her garden – cabbages and carrots and onions. She has flowers too. I don't know what they're for. She cuts them like the cabbages and brings them in; then after a few days she throws them out again without using them for anything.

When Martin found the bullocks going round and round the garden with Bark after them, he didn't know what to do. I had to help him for pity. We drove the cattle into the small yard by the road, and Martin slammed the gate and grabbed Bark's collar as he went by. All this time, a strange man was leaning on the wall watching.

'That black dog is good after cattle,' says he. 'Is he for sale?'

Martin isn't clever like the Boss, and he's always trying to do something to earn praise. Now he saw his chance. 'He's for sale,' says he, 'but the price is four hundred.'

'I'll buy,' says the man, 'if I get fifty pounds luck.'

Martin worked it out. 'All right so,' says he. The man wrote him a cheque for four hundred. 'You should've stopped the luck money out of it,' says Martin.

'Never do that,' says the man. 'It helps the taxman.' Martin went inside and brought out five ten-pound notes. The man took Bark and the money and drove away in his car.

Martin was in great humour for the rest of the week-end. The cheque was in his name, but the bank was shut until Monday. He meant to get the money all in tenners, so when Jim came back he'd be sure to give him one for very shame.

On Saturday he went to Coolcoffin and bought a big box of chocolates for his girlfriend. In the evening she came over to the farm and they ate them.

On Sunday, he went to a match.

Sunday night late the Boss and the Missis came home. Martin had gone to bed. I was never more pleased to see anyone.

In the morning, I heard the Boss and Martin talking.

'How could I tell the cheque was no good?' says Martin.

'Your own sense should have told you,' says the Boss. 'The cheque-book was stolen from someone's pocket at the races. What did your man look like?'

'He was a medium-sized man in a cap,' says Martin.

'Where was he from?'

'He didn't say.'

'Where was he going?'

'I didn't ask him.'

'What kind of car had he?' The Boss was getting angrier by the minute.

'It was either red or brown, I think. It might have been a Ford. Or maybe a Toyota,' says Martin. 'I didn't notice the number.'

Out comes the Missis then in a right state. 'There's fifty pounds gone out of the dresser,' says she.

So then Martin had to explain about the luck penny.

By the time the Boss had finished with him, I was real sorry for him. And then Jim arrived in a van he'd got a loan of because a tree had collided with his Mini on the Lisdoonvarna road. He wasn't as mad as the Boss because he had a dislike taken to Bark, and he had to admit he'd talked Martin into minding him and Taff. He said he wanted no payment; he'd take a pup sometime.

The talk is that the man belongs to a gang of sheep-stealers. If he goes stealing sheep with Bark, he'll soon be caught. Bark likes to be noticed, and he must be the noisiest dog in Ireland.

WIDE-EYED

I've been seeing life this week. Mixing with criminals and all. This was the way of it.

Mr O'Brien told the Boss that when he brought Tiny over for training he could bring me too if he liked and spend the day gathering sheep in the hills. There's thousands of them up there, and some people get money for taking their dogs and going to help.

The first man I saw when we got out of the car was Chris, who wanted to buy Tiny at the dog sale. He had a white sheepdog with him: at least she was meant to be white. She told me she was called Floosie.

'What's your name?' says she to me.

'I'm Shep,' says I proudly, 'and I won on the telly.'

'Oh, I know you now,' says Floosie. 'You do the ad for the worm dose. "No parasites now, says Shep, thanks to Vermolin."'

I was ashamed. I said nothing.

'Don't mind me,' says Floosie, quite kindly. 'I may be a sheep-killer, but I'm well-connected and I wish I'd had your chances, so I do.'

Just then we had to set off up the hill and start work, and I got no more talk with her for an hour or two. Then I said, 'What did you mean, a sheep-killer? That's murder: you get shot for it.'

'I know that,' says Floosie, cheerfully, 'none better.

And I'm such a good target too, all white. Yes, I've helped to kill dozens of sheep, rounding them up for the gang. That was near Dublin.'

Most of us sheepdogs are related and I didn't want to admit to being related to a murderess, so I said, 'You are purebred, aren't you?'

Floosie snarled. 'I am, of course,' says she. 'I'm Bally-bog Drift, number 113765, sold as a pup for a pet, I thank you, and reared in a Dublin flat. Now, are you satisfied? And I don't bring in the hens for the Missis neither, and I'm not let have any pups. Now shut your gob: you give me a pain.' She turned her back and started looking for fleas.

I got on with sorting the sheep, but me mind wasn't on the job at all. Floosie had such power and style. I could hardly believe her story. I says to her later, 'It's in the trials you should be.'

Floosie was still in a bad humour. She says, 'I might be a better dog than Finn there, even if he did come second in the intermediate class at Ballyjamesduff the year before last. You go home to the Missis and sit by the kitchen fire. You might get a rasher for your tea. Tiny's a better dog than you: if he'd been with the gang, we'd never have been hungry.' I was going to say something for Tiny, but he'd just pulled a big lump of wool off a sheep, so I kept quiet.

By the end of the day's work we were well tired out. Mr O'Brien took Tiny home with him. I rode home in the front of the car with the Boss for the first time in me life. He'd enjoyed the day, and was singing 'Spancilhill'.

When I got home I told Jess about Floosie. 'I know her sort,' says Jess. 'She's a white slave, that's what she is.'

ASHAMED

I'm in a right mess now, so I am, and it's me own fault as usual. The Boss and the Missis and Martin was all at a field evening in Coolcoffin and I was minding the house. Tiny is away being trained, and Jess was tied up.

A car stopped outside our gate, and that Chris jumped out and opened the boot. I stood on the doorstep, growling, but he didn't mind me. He left the boot lid up and got back in the car, leaving the door open.

I do like riding in cars so much – at least I did. I waited a bit, then I went and looked in. There was Floosie's dirty white face looking out.

'Hello Handsome,' says she.

'How are you going on?' says I, and I jumped in for a chat.

'You're a right eejit, Shep,' says Floosie.

'Why?' says I. The boot lid banged down.

'That's the why,' says Floosie.

The car started up and drove away. I scratched and whined, and Floosie says, 'Be quiet, will you? Do you want to bring my Boss around to us?'

'Is he cruel? Does he beat you?' I wanted to know.

'Not he,' says Floosie, 'he's too good a handler for that, but he'd beat us if it would make us work better. It's hard he is. No heart.'

'Why do you work for him so?' says I.

'Because I'm a dog, of course. Stop asking damnfool questions and go to sleep.' Floosie settled down to sleep herself, as the car drove on and on.

At last it stopped, and Chris opened the boot. We were in a locked yard. Floosie jumped out, and Chris tied her up in a shed. (There was another dog in there too.) Then he went away and fetched three dead rabbits. He threw two to Floosie and the other dog, and left one in the shed for me. I wasn't hungry. I sat in the doorway, wondering what would I do at all. I was thinking of my people coming home and missing me, the Missis crying, the Boss shouting for me and Martin maybe getting the Guards.

'I'd advise you to eat that rabbit,' says Floosie. 'We don't get fancy dogfood here. If Snap here doesn't catch any rabbits, we're lucky if we get fed every day.' I looked at Snap. You could call him a sheepdog if you were short-sighted, but his legs were twice as long as mine.

'I'm unique,' says Snap, 'if you know what that means. One of me grandfathers won the International and the other won the Waterloo Cup.' I was going to say I won on the telly, then I thought I'd better not.

After a while, a little lad about ten years of age came into the yard. He called me by name and patted me. I love children and I wagged me tail and licked his face. He put a twine through me collar, led me into the shed, chained me up, and shut the door. 'You soft old fool,' says Floosie. 'You've spent too long under the kitchen table. No wonder they codded you into selling worm pills.'

I was ashamed. I said nothing.

MISERABLE

I'm still here with Chris and his dogs, and I'm pure solid miserable. I have been working for Chris and I have helped him to steal sheep. Floosie says, 'Ah, you can't help yourself, Softy; you're a dog, like I said.'

I don't know what to make of Floosie. When she puts her head down on her paws and looks up at you sideways, she'd charm the heart out of a cabbage, but I can't keep up with her moods. Sometimes she'd call me Lover Boy or Dreamy Eyes, seeming real friendly and making me wish I wasn't tied on such a short chain. Other times, it's Softy or Flatfeet, and she's sneering at me. I don't understand one bit of her, so I don't. Snap sneers at me all the time, and I wouldn't eat the rabbits he catches if I got anything else.

Chris takes Floosie and me up on the hill every evening around dusk. We go in the car and he keeps me on a chain till we get to the sheep. Then I just seem to work for him, though he's ne'er a bit like the Boss. He has a squeaky voice and he smells of stale beer and cabbage and mice. My trouble is I'm not a one-man dog. I work for the Boss or the Missis, Martin or Mr O'Brien, and now I'm working for this squint-eyed blackguard, just like Floosie said I would. He even taught me a new command. When I get to the back of the sheep, he whistles like a curlew, and that means I'm to bring them. I do too.

The other night we went out late. The night was as black as the hob of hell. When we got to a lonesome place, we waited for the moon to come up, then we rounded up about a dozen sheep and loaded them in a trailer. I nearly died when Floosie told me we were stealing them. Even so, I know I'll help Chris steal some more if he asks me.

It's a dog's life, being a dog.

Yesterday we were locked up as usual when we heard a car. The next minute I heard Mr O'Brien talking to Chris. He was saying, 'Jack Kelly has lost Shep. I wonder...' I didn't hear any more, because Floosie and Snap began barking at the tops of their voices. I whined real loud, but no one could have heard me. They never stopped until the car had gone.

'We don't want to lose you, Softy,' says Floosie.

Chris has a friend called Joe. It was Joe that took the sheep we stole. He was here yesterday and him and Chris was talking about a 'big job'. It's to do with taking a whole flock of sheep off the hills. Chris is sure Mr O'Brien guesses that he has me here and why. He was in dread to go on with the job.

'All right so,' says Joe. 'I'll soon find a new partner with a couple of decent dogs, and you can do without your thousand pounds.' He was going away, but Chris called him back and said he'd take the chance.

Last night when I was chained up I sang the saddest song I know, 'The Kerry Blues'.

'Hold your whisht, will you,' says Floosie, 'or you'll get us all beaten. I heard Joe say that your Boss is offering a big reward for you. Think of that now! I was thrown out of a car and abandoned fifty miles from home by me own Boss. I was lucky Chris picked me up. Count your blessings, Softy,' says she.

HAPPY

I'm home! I'm back with the Boss and the Missis, lying under the kitchen table. (I mean I am, not the Boss and the Missis, of course.)

I was so happy, didn't I gallop three times round our yard, jumping at the swallows, like poor Dolly used to do. The Missis thought that all I went through must have turned me brain. I've had a bath and a big plate of my special food, which is called Collywobbles. There was such excitement here this morning when Mr O'Brien brought me home that Martin went to the creamery and forgot to take the milk, so he had to come back for it.

This is how I was rescued. Chris had it all fixed to get a whole lorry of sheep off the hill last night. He took me and Floosie up there in his car and we met Joe. Then we walked a nice bit to a clump of trees at the roadside. There was a lorry and trailer there.

It was black dark near the trees, but when we went out in the open we could see sheep scattered all over. Me and Floosie went around them, one each side, and when we heard Chris give his curlew whistle we fetched them to the lorry. We dogs knew well that there was people watching us not far off while we were loading the sheep, but nothing happened until Joe and Chris were both putting up the back of the lorry. Then suddenly there was Guards everywhere. They grabbed Joe and Chris and the lorry driver and held them fast. Then I saw Mr O'Brien was with them.

'Which dog is it you say was stolen? Can you prove it?' says one of the Guards.

'I can,' says Mr O'Brien, and he tells me to fetch the sheep out of the lorry again. I went straight in and fetched them out. Then I went and jumped up at him, which I am not allowed to do, but I forgot meself.

'That's proof enough,' says the Guard, 'you can take him with you.'

'Are you coming, Floosie?' says I.

'Not me,' says Floosie. 'I'll stick to this villain here. See you in prison, Softy,' says she.

This morning early Mr O'Brien took me home to Cool-coffin.

I was getting so mistrustful of people I was thinking maybe he has me stolen now, but at least he's better than the last feller. Then we turned into our own yard and there was the Missis at the door and she says, 'Oh Denis, indeed we're grateful for all your trouble, but I know in me own mind poor Shep is dead.' Then she saw me in the car, and I'll skip the next bit because I was embarrassed. I mean, I think the world an' all of the Missis, but how glad I was Floosie hadn't come along.

Next, out comes the Boss. He was only after getting up.

'There's £100 reward for you, Denis,' says he. 'You eejit, you, get down. It's worth every penny to get Shep back.'

'I want no money,' says Mr O'Brien. 'I have enough of a reward seeing him back with you again. He's in a terrible mess, but I didn't want to delay bringing him home.'

So Mr O'Brien stayed for breakfast and the Boss gave him whiskey and the Missis gave him cornflakes and scrambled eggs and tea. He said he never had such a breakfast in his life.

I sat under the kitchen table and scratched and scratched. They have a terrible breed of flea where I've been staying.

SURPRISED

If you read all me stories, you might think Coolcoffin is one of the most important places in Ireland. It isn't. I found that out when I was travelling for the TV series. Of course, I started travelling at six weeks old when I came here all the way from Wicklow in an orange box, but I don't remember anything about that except I was frightened.

The finest place near here is Galway city, and the Boss was there yesterday for a meeting, trying to get the Government to do something, I don't know what. They're not going to do it anyway.

The Missis came for the ride and so did I – they hardly let me out of their sight now.

There's a new place there called 'The Dog Shop' and the Missis took me there on a lead to buy me a new collar with a nameplate on it. When we got there, one of the shop ladies turned out to be Miss Cairngorm, who stayed with us last Christmas.

She was delighted to see the Missis, who had no idea she had the shop bought.

'I know you must be dying to see my precious Teazie again,' says Miss Cairngorm, and she calls him into the shop. It was easy to see that Teazie wasn't dying to see me again.

'I've got another dog now,' says Miss Cairngorm. 'Poor

thing, I picked it up straying on the road miles from anywhere. It's a pretty creature, but doesn't agree with my gorgeous boy.' (She meant Teazie-Weazie! Could you believe it?)

Then she goes to the door and says, 'Here, Blanche!' I nearly dropped when Floosie swaggered into the shop, clean and shining and wearing a tartan collar.

'Would you give her a good home?' asks Miss Cairngorm.

'I don't know,' says the Missis, 'I'd have to ask the Boss.'

'Hello, Dreamy,' says Floosie to me. 'I'll come with you this time if I get the chance. Old Lassie here is driving me crackers.'

'I am *not* called Lassie,' says Mr Teazie-Weazie. 'I keep telling you it's the breed. I was at Cruft's, I'd have you know, and I should have won. There's too much corruption nowadays.'

I was puzzled. I know what corruption is. It smells nice and you roll on it and then they won't let you into the house. I'm not sure what crufts are, but I think they might be small farms in Scotland.

'I won on the telly,' says I.

'Really?' says Teazie-Weazie. 'I don't watch the farming programmes, I'm afraid.'

Floosie lay down with her head on the Missis' foot and rolled her eyes up at her. That did it. Down went the Missis on the two knees.

'Isn't she a dote?' says she. 'I'll chance taking her, and bring her back to you if Jack kicks up. Will that do?' Then the Missis took us both to the car, where we waited anxiously for the Boss.

When he came, he started to give out about Floosie. Then he suddenly shut up and had a better look at her.

'Well, there's justice for you,' says he. 'I'll take me Bible oath that's Chris's Floosie.'

'Her name's Blanche,' says the Missis.

'Blanche, where are ye,' says the Boss. 'She's Floosie, one of the best dogs in the West. We'll keep her all right, and I'll buy you a present before we go.' He sang 'Spancilhill' all the way home.

I wonder how will Floosie and Jess get on.

TIPSY

Floosie and Jess don't agree at all, so they don't. I was afraid of it. In fact, Jess isn't talking to me at all, because she blames me for bringing Floosie here. When I asked Floosie why wouldn't she settle down here with me and Jess and have some pups to help occupy her time, she showed all her beautiful white teeth in what might have been a smile and didn't bother answering me.

'Don't you like puppies, Floosie?' says I.

'Love 'em,' says Floosie. 'I had seven half-spaniel puppies once. They died young, poor little things. I don't care to talk about it.'

'Give you half a chance and you'll be worrying sheep again,' says Jess.

'I will not then,' says Floosie. 'I'm anti-blood sports now. I'll be going when Chris comes out of prison though. I don't like your Boss: he knows more about a plate of bacon and cabbage than he does about a sheep-dog. Besides, he sings out of tune.'

I don't like quarrelling, so I stay in the house as much as I am let.

Martin and Julia are married now. He kept putting it off for one reason or another, so the Missis told him to get on with it and they got married last week. They're going to live in a new house down the road as soon as they finish building it. They're living here at present.

The wedding was great gas. Martin went to Galway to get a suit and forgot, and came home without it.

The Missis says, 'You can't be married in a pullover and jeans or a tracksuit.'

'Why not?' says Martin. He had to borrow a suit from his cousin, Dan. Martin and Dan isn't the same size, but even so.

I didn't see the wedding service in Galway because I was in the car boot, but I did go to the party afterwards in the big hotel. Floosie was to go too, because Julia is mad about her, and she said they'd have their photos took together. However, the Boss took the notion to shift the bullocks out of the silage pit with her the same morning, so she had to stay at home.

The wedding party was a little like the big dinner I was at in England but much noisier, and there was a dance after it. The Boss had a new song learned. It is called 'Lanigan's Ball' and I like it much better than 'Spancilhill'. He sang it twice and he danced with Julia till Martin got fed up and went off to the bar. I stopped with the Missis and her sister and Julia's Mammy.

The party went on till night. I got a plate of chicken and ham to eat. Then I went to sleep. When I woke I was on me own, so I went out to the door and saw Martin and Julia driving off in our car. I didn't see the Boss with the crowd that was in it, so I thought they were leaving me after them, and I ran out onto the road. I missed getting run over by a whisker. Me blood runs cold when I think of it. The Boss was there all the time: he had drink taken and forgot about me.

He came straight after me, in among all the cars, and I saw him and went to him. Some of the cars ran into each other; you could hear breaking glass and bad language. I went back into the hotel with the Boss, leaving them to sort themselves out. Someone gave me some stout to drink; I don't think it's all it's cracked up to be.

I don't remember coming home.

When Martin and Julia's house is finished, Floosie is going to live with them. This will be a good thing for me and Jess, and when I have some peace again I might think about writing another book.

That's all I have to say this time.

Shep, Coolcoffin, 1984